table for two

*For Tracy!
happy cooking*

[signature]

table for two

COOKING AND ENTERTAINING FOR YOU AND YOUR +1

written & photographed by

marc j. sievers

MARC-RYAN GROUP
CHICAGO

Copyright © 2016 by Marc J. Sievers
All rights reserved. Published 2016.

Cover and book design, layout, and photographs of Marc, by Ryan L. Sievers

Marc J. Sievers is also the author of *Entertaining with Love—Inspired recipes for everyday entertaining*

Visit Marc's website: marcsievers.com

No part of this book may be reproduced in any form or by any electronic or mechanical means, including information storage and retrieval systems, without permission in writing from the author, except by a reviewer who may quote brief passages in a review.

While the publisher and author have used their best efforts in preparing this book, they make no representations or warranties with respect to the accuracy or completeness of the contents of this book and specifically disclaim any implied warranties of merchantability or fitness for a particular purpose. The advice and strategies contained herein may not be suitable for your situation. Neither the publisher nor the author shall be liable for any loss or damages, including but not limited to special, incidental, consequential, or other damages. Always use your best judgment and be safe in and around your kitchen.

Published in the United States by Marc-Ryan Group
Chicago Illinois USA
Visit our website: marc-ryan.com

First Edition: November 2016

Sievers, Marc J.
Table for Two: Cooking and entertaining for you and your +1 / Marc J. Sievers – 1st ed.
Includes recipe index.

ISBN-13: 978-0-692-75468-9
ISBN-10: 0-692-75468-7

American made. Printed in the United States of America | 2

The name Marc-Ryan Group, the stylized 'RM' symbol, and the 'RM' circle symbol are trademarks or registered trademarks of Marc-Ryan Group, Chicago USA. The name Marc Sievers and the stylized lowercase 'marc' and uppercase 'sievers' symbol, and the lowercase 'm' and orange underline are trademarks or registered trademarks of Marc-Ryan Group, Chicago USA.

At the time of publication: The name Le Creuset and its trade dress are trademarks or registered trademarks of Le Creuset S.A.S., Fresnoy le Grand France. The name St-Germain and its trade dress are trademarks or registered trademarks of Bacardi Limited, Bermuda. The name Calphalon and its trade dress are trademarks or registered trademarks of Calphalon Corporation, Atlanta USA. The name Grand Marnier and its trade dress are trademarks or registered trademarks of Société des Produits Marnier Lapostolle, Paris France. All other marks are trademarks of their respective owners.

I dedicate this book to my nan, who passed away in August 2015. She always encouraged me to be me, fostered my creativity in the kitchen, and was ready and willing to hop in my little red wagon and race with me to the next adventure. Nan, you will always and forever be my original +1.

Thanks!

BEATRICE & FRANK
From the moment I fell at your feet, we were destined for a lifetime of friendship, laughter, and love

JOYCE
I will forever cherish your joie de vie and marvelous stories of a lifetime—you inspire me to be true to myself

ROBERT
You are old-school, kind-hearted, incredibly stylish, and inspire me to always set a fabulous table, darling

JENN
My first true +1 in Chicago—and always Lady's preferred +1—your laugh and friendship means the world to me

LINDA
You are a fabulous artist, photographer, and friend—I adore your spirit, and love of adventure and food

RYAN
Me and you, just us two

WITH ALL MY LOVE,

Marc
xo

TABLE OF CONTENTS

Introduction
11

How to Use This Book
23
YOUR GUIDE TO COOKING AND ENTERTAINING FOR TWO

- 26 — SHOPPING FOR TWO – *How to shop effectively for two*
- 29 — EVERYDAY INGREDIENTS & INDEX – *What to have on hand for you and a +1*
- 35 — KITCHEN EQUIPMENT – *Simple kitchen tools to make recipes for two*

Entertaining for Two
37
STYLES AND MENUS FOR ENTERTAINING AT HOME

- 39 — COFFEE TABLE – *Cocktails and nibbles*
- 43 — KITCHEN ISLAND – *Cooking and entertaining together*
- 47 — DINING TABLE – *An updated classic*
- 51 — IN BED – *In-bed fête*
- 55 — TV TRAYS – *Not your average TV dinner*

Recipes for Two
59
EASY AND ELEGANT VEGETARIAN COOKING

- 61 — GOOD MORNING – *Delicious recipes for a simple and chic breakfast or brunch*
- 83 — HORS D'OEUVRE & COCKTAILS – *Cocktails and nibbles perfected for two*
- 125 — SOUPS & SALADS – *Fresh and flavorful first courses*
- 145 — SIDES – *Fabulous dishes to compliment any menu*
- 169 — MAIN COURSES – *Perfectly portioned for you and your +1*
- 209 — DESSERTS – *The perfect ending for any occasion*

Recipe Index
235

Notes & Guest Book
239

Introduction

"Regardless of what Andy Warhol said, two is a party! And this book is for exactly that—for you and your +1, whoever that may be, and for any occasion. Do two people ever really need any more of a reason for a party than simply being together?!"
—Marc J. Sievers

INTRODUCTION

I used to think that cooking for two elegantly was just too difficult and time consuming. Throwing a dinner party for four people, eight, or even twenty people for a cocktail party, was something I could do easily. But, cooking for two often proved more of a challenge when it came to preparation and scale. I think most of us are programmed for the bigger events. I grew up with family and friends coming and going like it was Grand Central. Regardless of the day, week, or occasion, there was always something happening with a group of us. And those were definitely the highlights, filled with laughter, family, friends, and full stomachs! These days, it is fun and fabulous dinner parties with friends and family, and cocktail soirées with colleagues.

But what about cooking for two people? Really cooking for just two. As much fun as we have hosting (and being invited to!) dinner parties, they're not an every-night occurrence. When I really started to think about it, I actually spend quite a lot of time just me plus one. Of course, there's me and Ryan, but also colleagues, BFFs, neighbors, and so many other people I spend time with in a one-on-one setting at home. It also occurred to me that I was already adapting much of my approach to cooking and entertaining for two, but just not consciously recognizing it.

Cooking for two is more than just making a recipe that serves four, and doling out two servings (with left-overs to deal with). Entertaining for two is also more than just setting out two place settings where you would normally have parked four or six. And so that left the question of how to cook and entertain elegantly, but still keep things simple, flavorful, and familiar? How do you avoid making yourself crazy with preparation, as if you may as well be throwing a dinner party for six? This book is my answer to truly effortless cooking and entertaining, perfectly portioned and planned for two, laid out as an easy-to-follow guide.

As I began outlining *Table for Two*, the ideas were there, and the vision was starting to come together. I even did an initial test of a few recipes, and not long after that, I literally said out loud, "Oh, fuck!" For my first cookbook *Entertaining with Love*, Ryan was with me every step of the way, from planning, to helping me clean in between recipe testing days. He took every photograph, and coached me through how to write a book. This time, I was determined to take what I learned and lead every part of producing *Table for Two*. How hard could it be?! I was going to have to shop, test, take every photograph, clean,

m

Nan's kitchen—where I grew up and learned how to cook. I took this photo in 7th grade for my photography class. It hangs in my kitchen today.

INTRODUCTION

write, re-test, clean some more, and then hope that everything I was doing would result in something that resembled a cookbook!

As it turned out, it was a bit harder and scarier than I thought it would be! I wasn't a food stylist or a photographer. Sure, I take my own photos for my website and blog, but a book? An entire cookbook?! It seemed so much easier the first time. After being fortified with a few bottles of wine and chatting it over with Ryan one evening, I was *re*-convinced I could do it! For the most part, the process was creative, delicious, and enlightening. Of course, there were days I wanted to throw my camera out of the window, light my kitchen on fire, and just drink Champagne! In the end, I may not have burned down my kitchen, or smashed my camera, but there were days that the pop of a Champagne cork was heard before 10:00am (and not as a photo prop!). And so, like that, and in so many other wonderful moments, it came together. This book is really a reflection of me, my voice, and my vision for what I think elegant vegetarian cooking and stylish home entertaining can be.

Nan's kitchen where I grew up learning to cook (as did many of my cousins) was a very simple space. It wasn't filled with French cookware, marble countertops, or even sharp knives. It was however filled with love! She spent a lot of time in her kitchen, cooking for her family every day, on holidays, birthdays, and every imaginable occasion in between. Looking back, there weren't really any boundaries I couldn't cross to help out. Nan would even let me put the freshly cut potatoes in hot oil (I've *always* loved French fries!), guiding me and letting me learn.

In hindsight, it was probably better to have me doing something than just be underfoot. But it was in that "doing," those experiences, that left me wanting to learn more in the kitchen, and made it feel like a natural place to be. That was more foundational than I realized until I wrote my first cookbook. Experimenting in the kitchen on the scale needed to write an entire book was a hefty undertaking, but I reveled in it. My kitchen is my workshop, and I love to experiment and keep trying until I arrive at the dish exactly as I had it in my head. Comfort and confidence were key to both getting started and pushing through (sometimes a difficult thing when you watch a pound of lumpy grey chocolate slowly slide into the garbage can).

It wasn't until later in life that I realized not everyone had the same foundational experience in the

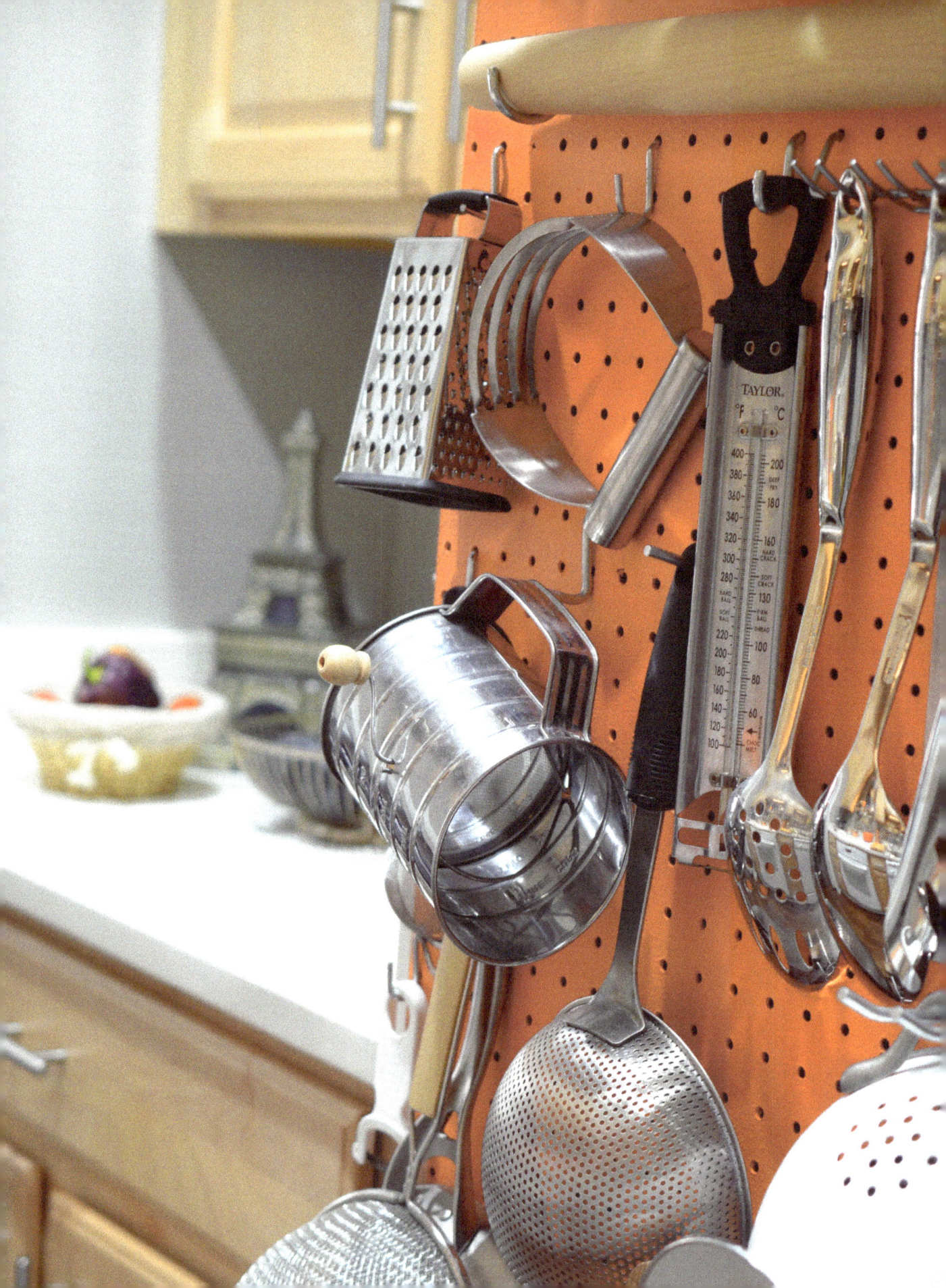

INTRODUCTION

kitchen as I did as a kid. There is saying, "I'm such a bad cook that I can burn water," that I actually saw in action with a friend in Chicago. When I wrote my first cookbook I adopted a philosophy of keeping things as simple as they could be, both in terms of the technique required to cook, but also in how easy the recipe itself was to read and follow. I wanted to convey that sense of comfort and confidence I had to my readers that they could then carry with them into the kitchen.

With *Table for Two*, I wanted to go beyond the standard cookbook format to cover a more holistic experience across food, socializing, and entertaining. Especially in a setting just for two, I feel it is important to show your +1 that you have made an effort just for them. But, entertaining for two simply shouldn't be as much of an effort as a dinner party for ten! In this book I have directly connected my recipes to the entertaining experience to help bridge the gap we often have when we need to scale down.

All this came about in a rather funny moment with Ryan. We love to throw fabulous dinner parties, and have fun with different dishes, themes, over-the-top flowers, incredible music, and so on. But for evenings we weren't entertaining, we had to choose between going out to a favorite neighborhood haunt, ordering in, or making dinner. Quite often, following a week of recipe testing, client projects, and other engagements, I would make the same thing over and over again—it was just easy. One night, as we were sitting on the sofa drinking wine (we never get tired of that course!), I excused myself to go make dinner, meaning re-heat leftover soup! Once I revealed what our exciting dinner was that fateful evening, Ryan finally exclaimed, "Don't you write recipes for a living? Don't you teach people how to entertain elegantly? Why are we always eating soup?!" And that was it! This book had to happen. For me, for you, for us all!

So what have you signed up for with *Table for Two*? This book is sticky with my finger prints! I wrote this book as part cookbook, part entertaining guide, and part memoire. Like for all of us, my perspective is driven by experiences and memories, and so I have shared my inspiration for recipes, experiences that have worked for me (and didn't!), and other anecdotes that hopefully give you a bit more of a personal connection to me, my work, and my perspective than just a clinical set of instructions to recreate a dish in your kitchen (that last part was in a robot voice).

I took all the photographs in this book (except for the few of me that Ryan reprised his role as

INTRODUCTION

photographer to capture). Frankly, my photography is untrained. Ryan showed me the ropes a few years back and as I have practiced and played around, I have figured out how to capture the imagine I have in my mind. Sometimes it was incredibly easy and done in just one shot, and other times I was imagining my camera resting peacefully at the bottom of Lake Michigan just to end the torture. Every photograph in this book is of the real dish, photographed in all-natural light, unedited or color-corrected, in my home (or a +1's), and was done in real-time as each final test of the recipe was finished. In my opinion, flavorful food is not about styling, it is about using and highlighting really fresh and flavorful ingredients. I wanted that to come through clearly in my photography (no motor oil or glue was used in the photography of this book!).

Similarly to my philosophy on photography, my entertaining ideas and vignettes are easy to re-create, and are meant to be a guide of inspiration to hopefully spark your inner home-entertaining voice! As you look through the entertaining section and photos, just imagine me wearing my satin pajamas, with chic French music blaring in the background, decked out in cocktail rings, prepping for the arrival of my +1, and a party of two about to begin! That is as real as it gets, dahling!

You don't need to be a wiz in the kitchen, or even an experienced host/ess to entertain at home. What you must be is willing! Willing to not only learn about fresh ingredients and useful techniques, but also to share that with your +1 and make whoever it is feel as through in that moment they are the only other person in the world that matters! Call up your +1, set a date, and use this fabulous guide to bring it all together!

HOW TO USE THIS BOOK

How to Use This Book
YOUR GUIDE TO COOKING AND ENTERTAINING FOR TWO

When I had the idea to write my first cookbook Entertaining with Love, I knew I wanted my recipes to be laid out more functionally than the typical cookbook. My goal was to create a cookbook that was genuinely easy-to-use so there would be as few barriers as possible between one of my recipes on a page and the finished dish on a reader's dining table. Here in Table for Two I have gone beyond the simple recipe to create a fabulous guide with dedicated sections about shopping for two, kitchen equipment, everyday ingredients, and how to entertain you and your +1.

SHOPPING FOR TWO
How to shop effectively for two

EVERYDAY INGREDIENTS & INDEX
What to have on hand for you and a +1

KITCHEN EQUIPMENT
Simple kitchen tools to make recipes for two

HOW TO USE THIS BOOK

Getting the Most from *Table for Two*
FOLLOWING THE METHOD TO MY MADNESS

I created this book with a complete party for two in mind! It begins with menu planning and shopping, then prep and cooking in the kitchen, and ending with a fabulous setting for you and your +1. In this section, **How to Use This Book**, I created dedicated segments to walk you through how to shop for two (an essential feature of this book), the kitchen equipment that will be useful for cooking from this book (and in general), and everyday ingredients (including an ingredient index) to help you plan recipes and ensure your kitchen has the staples needed for savvy home cooking. Further on, in **Entertaining for Two**, I laid out five vignettes for entertaining, along with menu options for each, to help give you some direction and inspiration for a party of two. And lastly, in **Recipes for Two**, I have created easy and elegant vegetarian recipes that use a smaller amount of ingredients, just for you and your +1, so you aren't managing leftovers of a dish for a week!

As you glance through the recipes of *Table for Two*, you will see a purposeful layout. Before I wrote *Entertaining with Love*, I had too many experiences in other recipes with key ingredients being buried in measurements, or instructional text, resulting in emergency runs to the grocery store only after it was discovered missing, at about two-thirds of the way through a recipe, while pots were gurgling away on the stove! For my first cookbook, Ryan and I brainstormed and designed different types of page layouts, aiming for a more straight-forward way of presenting the flow of the three parts that make up any recipe: Ingredients (the stuff), preparation (what you do to the stuff), and directions (how you put the stuff together). I have further refined my recipe layout in *Table for Two*, here are a few highlights:

Each recipe is laid out with a list of ① ingredients and preparation notes at the top right side of the page. Each ingredient is ② listed in the order that it appears in the directions of the recipe, and is ③ presented in a bolder type. Immediately following the ingredient is the ④ measurement needed, the way to prepare it (finely minced, diced, etc.), followed by any specific note or recommendations in parenthesis (Italian flat leaf parsley recommended). You can easily ⑤ make shopping lists by seeing the ingredients that are called for without having it buried in "¼ cup of diced yellow onion". Instead, you see "**Yellow Onion** - ¼ cup, ½-inch diced". Take a photo of the ingredients section with your smartphone and head to the grocery store with a clear list already made for you!

The recipe directions have ⑥ numbered steps to help you keep track of your progress through the cooking process. Some recipes have multiple components and those are separated clearly to help you navigate each part. Below the directions are ⑦ tips and ideas for preparation or cooking that go beyond the immediate directions for making the recipe. I have also included ⑧ little stories or food for thought for more about the recipe, my inspiration, or other anecdotes that I wanted to share with you. Lastly, for almost all the recipes, I have included a ⑨ space for notes for you to capture any adjustments or ideas you had while making the recipe, to help make it your own!

HOW TO USE THIS BOOK

Shopping for Two
HOW TO SHOP EFFECTIVELY FOR TWO

Shopping for two, if you are not used to doing so, may take some adjustment to your normal grocery store routine. It really begins with planning out your menu, but not for a week's worth of meals. The recipes in this cookbook call for smaller amounts of ingredients, most of which are fresh. I find that planning a day or two ahead and making more frequent trips to the grocery store (like they do in Paris!) to buy items as I need them has a few advantages. I am more focused with the need for what I am planning to make (instead of trying to buy ingredients based on the possibility of making any kind of random dinner throughout the week). Also, I use most everything I buy (so much less food waste!). Those two advantages have led me to actually spend a bit less as I buy only what I am going to use, and not wasting what I don't need, or didn't have time to use!

There are so many options for people to shop for groceries now. The larger grocery store chains are doing more and more to keep up with and cater to us, the savvy home cooks. Technology is trying to keep pace, too. Mobile apps and online delivery services are making it ever-easier to stock our pantries with staples. Altogether, these options are offering more fresh, local, and organic produce. In recent years, grocers have been greatly improving and expanding their bulk sections, where you can buy rice, grains, legumes, flours, pasta, beans, dried fruits, nuts, seeds, spices, teas and coffee, each sold by weight.

In my mind, "bulk" is not in reference to those gigantic warehouse stores where you take home a bushel of tomatoes, a carton of 96 eggs, or a 2-gallon container of mayonnaise! I mean bulk where you can scoop and weigh out either the exact amount you need for a recipe – like French lentils – or just smaller amounts in general. This approach ensures you use what you buy, and buy only what you plan to use. That is an important consideration for having fresh ingredients on hand. It also helps with storage space. No one needs a 5-gallon barrel of pickles stored next to their laundry detergent that lasts for ten years!

Use these additional tips, shopping ideas, and storage tricks to help ensure your grocery store trips result in fresh, flavorful, and fabulous ingredients:

1. In the bulk section of your grocery store, buy just what you need to make sure that you don't end up with uselessly-small amounts leftover and sitting in your cupboard or pantry, losing freshness and wasting space.

2. If you can't buy in the form of bulk, transfer all leftover dried goods to glass jars and store in a cool dry place. I really think that even dried goods have a shelf life. So use them up within a few months to ensure your meals have as much flavor as possible.

HOW TO USE THIS BOOK

③ Because of their high oil content, nuts can go rancid very quickly. I store mine in the refrigerator in glass containers. I think they stay fresher, longer. But, I still make an effort to use them within a few months after purchasing them.

④ Change the function of those crisper draws at the bottom of your fridge (fresh produce just disappears into an abyss!). Remove them completely and line the base with a rubberized mat to store bottles of Champagne, white wine, and other bottled beverages.

⑤ With the crisper drawers gone, keep your fresh vegetables, herbs, and fruits stored on line-of-sight shelves, making it easier to "shop" your own refrigerator.

⑥ Organize all the other "stuff" that shares the shelves with your produce, by grouping bottles of condiments, cheeses, and other items in clear refrigerator-safe plastic bins. This allows you to pull out a whole group of items and rummage through them with the refrigerator door closed. The bins will also save you from the unwieldy messes that can happen with refrigerator shelves, and the dreaded "lost bottles" or "mystery cheese" that are only ever found again when then they break, stink, or you move!

⑦ Buy softer cheeses and stinky cheeses in smaller sizes. The cheese monger or deli department will happily cut an already portioned amount of cheese into your desired size. I store these types of cheeses in special cheese paper from France that has a wax-coating and allows cheese to breathe, helps regulate humidity, and ultimately keeps cheese fresher. Smaller quantities will ensure that you get the full flavor benefit from your cheese.

⑧ To keep basil fresh for as long as possible, trim the stems as you would flowers to remove dried-up ends, then place the bunch in a tall glass of water. Loosely cover the basil with a plastic bag (like a gallon-sized Ziploc bag) and keep it on the counter and out of the sun.

HOW TO USE THIS BOOK

Everyday Ingredients
WHAT TO HAVE ON HAND FOR YOU AND A +1

Ingredients go hand-in-hand with shopping, but involve a bit more planning. In essence, this is about preparing your pantry and refrigerator with what to have on hand that is fresh, what you should have at the ready, and what special or unique ingredients will require a trip to the store. When I think of everyday ingredients, I think of items that can be found in a typical grocery store. It drives me nuts when I read a recipe that calls for some obscure ingredient that I then have to run around the city to find in a specialty store! It used to be like that to find saffron, truffle oil, and even certain cheeses. Now, a great number of grocery stores (and even online delivery services) are doing a fabulous job of stocking a very wide array of ingredients, and from around the world. This has made savvy home cooking a much easier and more flavorful experience! If you can't find a particular ingredient, ask the store to order it for you, or shop online.

When I was growing up, fresh herbs in particular, were not as abundantly found as they are now. I rely so much on fresh herbs in my cooking as they really do add so much more flavor, color, and texture to recipes than dried herbs. In addition to using fresh herbs, I also use familiar fruits, vegetables, pantry items, cheeses, and other ingredients to help support flavorful, easy, and elegant vegetarian home cooking.

In this section, I have provided a complete list of every ingredient used in this cookbook, all categorized by type, and along with the page numbers for all recipes where each ingredient is used. Because each recipe calls for smaller amounts and measurements, you can look for each ingredient (for example, basil) to see what pages it appears on and also find another recipe where you can use the remainder of basil. You can also use the index of ingredients to look up what you already have on hand (maybe a small amount of crème fraîche leftover), find inspiration after a trip to a farmer's market (I always overbuy!), have an abundant garden, or when you want to try a new ingredient you've never cooked with!

Now, don't be put off by the very long list of ingredients (208 to be exact!) that I used in this book! I am not suggesting that you have to run out and buy everything on the list all at once. In fact, as you start to cook your way through this book (or if you cook on a regular basis), you will automatically build up a stocked kitchen of ingredients, especially things like flour, sugar, honey, Dijon mustard, etc., and other things that are kept in your pantry, stored in the refrigerator, and freezer. You will have to

HOW TO USE THIS BOOK

continually buy your fresh ingredients like dairy, cheese, herbs, vegetables, etc., but that is where the fun part begins! A majority of this book (and my cooking) uses the same cast of characters over and over again, but layered and paired in different ways to create new flavor profiles, interesting textures, and ultimately a fabulous finished dish – I mean, who wants bland food?!

The only ingredients I did not include in the index are butter, sea salt, black pepper, and olive oil. These appear in so many of the recipes as foundational ingredients that it would not be particularly useful to flag every page in which they appear. However, because these four ingredients make such an incredible difference and are essential to savvy home cooking, I elaborated on each a little further:

Butter - I use unsalted butter so I can control the amount of salt in my cooking and baking. I prefer French butter, as it is a world of difference in flavor (and color), but it can be pricey, and so I tend to use it in baking when I really want to up the flavor. (I wrote this cookbook using unsalted American butter.)

Sea Salt - I use coarse sea salt in all of my cooking and baking. It is a bit softer on the palette and also adds a little texture, particularly when using it to season a finished a dish.

Black Pepper - I always use freshly cracked black pepper. Investing in a good pepper mill (one that allows you to adjust coarseness) is an essential step in elevating your cooking. Freshly cracked black pepper has a wonderfully rich layer of flavors that is simply missing in the nearly-powered stuff in a shaker.

Olive Oil - My favorite olive oil to keep on hand for cooking is a fresh and fruity extra virgin olive oil that has pronounced fruit flavors, pungency, pepperiness, and body. This type of olive oil will blend well with the flavors of most any dish, without overpowering it, while still adding flavor and richness. Expensive doesn't always mean it is better, so taste a few and find one that works well for your palette.

HOW TO USE THIS BOOK

Ingredients Index
EACH INGREDIENT IN *TABLE FOR TWO* BY CATEGORY

BEANS, LEGUMES, & PASTA
Black Beans – 131, 195
Cannellini Beans – 119, 143, 177, 187
Chickpeas – 113
Elbow Macaroni – 175
Fettuccini – 189
French Green Lentils – 135, 185
Italian Arborio Rice – 183, 199
Orzo – 159
Quinoa – 195
Rice Noodles – 207
Tofu – 207

BREAD
Baguette – 87, 127
Challah Bread – 203
Cinnamon Raisin Bread – 69, 179
Croissant – 81, 223
Dried Bread Crumbs – 101, 177, 187
French Boule – 107, 121, 139
Panko Bread Flakes – 175
Pretzel Slider Buns – 177

CONDIMENTS & GARNISHES
Blue Cheese Stuffed Olives – 101
Capers – 199
Cerignola Olives – 191
Dijon Mustard – 133, 177, 181
Sriracha Hot Chili Sauce – 207
Tabasco Sauce – 123
Thai Chili Garlic Paste – 189
Wasabi Peas – 97, 189

DAIRY & CHEESE
Blue Cheese – 111, 137, 147
Boursin® Cheese – 63
Camembert Cheese – 89
Crème Fraîche – 107, 129, 133, 147, 157, 159, 179, 195, 205, 215, 217
Eggs – 63, 65, 69, 73, 75, 81, 101, 133, 155, 171, 177, 181, 187, 197, 203, 215, 219, 231
Fontina Cheese – 87, 175, 203
French Feta Cheese – 141
Fresh Mozzarella Cheese – 143
Goat Cheese – 99, 191, 205
Gorgonzola Cheese – 183
Gruyère Cheese – 81, 167, 171, 177, 181
Half & Half – 69, 73, 139, 147, 155, 157, 175, 177, 179, 181, 187, 201, 205
Heavy Cream – 63, 75, 79, 105, 167, 183, 211, 215, 217, 221, 225, 229
Mascarpone Cheese – 69, 81, 191, 217, 221
Mayonnaise – 123, 147, 177
Paneer Cheese – 201
Parmesan Cheese – 63, 81, 87, 93, 119, 127, 129, 131, 143, 151, 153, 155, 157, 159, 171, 173, 177, 179, 183, 185, 187, 191, 195
Pecorino Cheese – 181, 203
Pepper Jack Cheese – 197
Plain Greek Yogurt – 93, 123
Port Salut Cheese – 193
Triple Cream Brie Cheese – 121, 165, 179
White Cheddar Cheese – 155, 175
Whole Milk – 65, 105, 197

FRESH HERBS
Basil – 67, 91, 119, 121, 127, 147, 151, 159, 163, 165, 177, 185, 187, 189, 193, 195, 205, 207
Chives – 107, 111, 137, 143, 181, 195, 205
Dill – 107, 123, 153, 185
Parsley – 63, 87, 93, 103, 123, 127, 135, 147, 157, 159, 161, 171, 177, 181, 183, 185, 187, 195, 199, 201
Rosemary – 109, 131, 141, 143, 165, 177, 181, 187, 191
Scallions – 93, 123, 139, 147, 189, 197, 199, 205, 207
Thyme – 131, 135, 143, 155, 167, 171, 175, 177, 179, 181, 187, 197

FROZEN
Edamame – 115
Frozen Berry Medley – 67, 227
Green Peas – 107, 199, 201
Puff Pastry – 89, 171, 193
Raspberry Sorbet – 227

FRUITS
Avocado – 97, 189
Banana – 65, 233
Bartlett Pear – 193, 195
D'Anjou Pear – 89
Granny Smith Apple – 67, 69, 137, 147, 179, 185
Green Grapes – 141
Lemon – 71, 73, 85, 91, 105, 107, 111, 123, 137, 159, 161, 177, 181, 183, 185, 199, 215, 227
Lime – 85, 97, 117, 189, 205, 207
Orange – 67, 69, 191, 195, 219

HOW TO USE THIS BOOK

FRUITS (CONTINUED)
Peach - 109, 141, 221
Pineapple - 217
Pink Lady Apple - 171
Plum - 141, 221
Raspberries - 95, 221
Red Grapes - 141
Strawberries - 73, 151

LIQUOR
Amaretto - 85, 95
Chambord® - 95, 227
Champagne - 91, 95, 109, 227
Dark Rum - 217
Gin - 91
Grand Marnier® - 95, 231
Luxardo® Maraschino - 95
Rosé - 109
Silver Tequila - 117
St-Germain® - 95, 117
Triple Sec - 109
White Wine - 199

NUTS & DRIED FRUITS
Candied Orange Peel - 231
Dried Black Mission Figs - 75, 159, 179
Dried Blueberries - 77
Dried Coconut Chips - 97
Dried Cranberries - 137
Dried Mango Slices - 77, 97
Dried Tart Cherries - 77, 231

Golden Raisins - 147, 171
Pecans - 141
Pine Nuts - 153
Pistachios - 99, 137
Raisins - 69
Raw Cashews - 77, 171
Raw Pumpkin Seeds - 77
Sliced Almonds - 93
Sweetened Shredded Coconut - 213
Toasted Coconut Almonds - 77

PANTRY ITEMS
Apple Cider Vinegar - 137
Baking Powder - 73, 75, 219, 233
Baking Soda - 73
Balsamic Vinegar - 119, 141, 149, 151
Balsamic Vinegar Reduction - 193
Canola Oil - 77, 101, 133, 181, 207
Champagne Vinegar - 133, 147
Cocoa Powder - 231
Coconut Milk - 189
Corn Starch - 207
Dark Brown Sugar - 211, 217, 221
Earl Grey Tea - 71, 79
Fig Preserves - 99, 179
Fire Roasted Tomatoes - 201
Flour - 65, 73, 75, 155, 167, 175, 197, 213, 219, 221, 231
Graham Crackers - 223
Honey - 65, 69, 71, 77, 79, 85, 109, 137, 141, 157, 165, 181, 193, 201, 213, 215, 217, 221, 225, 233

Maple Syrup - 65, 69, 89, 219
Marinated Artichoke Hearts - 127
Mini Marshmallows - 223
Old-Fashioned Rolled Oats - 77, 221
Peanut Butter - 233
Popcorn - 103
Powdered Sugar - 65, 219, 231
Raspberry Preserves - 227
Roasted Red Peppers - 63
Salt & Pepper Potato Chips - 111
Semi-Sweet Chocolate - 223, 231
Shortbread Cookies - 225
Sugar - 67, 73, 75, 175, 215, 221, 229
Sugar Cubes - 95
Sun Dried Tomatoes - 119
Superfine Sugar - 91, 109
Sweetened Condensed Milk - 213
Taco Shells - 205
Tomato Paste - 199
Truffle Oil - 203
Vanilla - 65, 69, 211, 213, 215, 219, 229, 231
Vanilla Bean Paste - 225
Vegetable Stock - 129, 131, 135, 139, 183, 199, 207, 233
Vodka Sauce - 87
White Chocolate - 225
Whole Wheat Flour - 233

HOW TO USE THIS BOOK

SPICES

Bay Leaf - 185

Black Sesame Seeds - 97

Cayenne Pepper - 113, 205

Chili Powder - 205

Chipotle Pepper - 205

Cinnamon - 69, 137, 225

Cumin - 201, 205

Dried Lavender - 79

Fleur de Sel - 71, 99, 103, 117, 153, 193, 211, 223, 225

Garlic Powder - 113

Herbes de Provence - 103, 139, 161

Nutmeg - 69, 167

Oregano - 87, 159, 177, 187

Red Pepper Flakes - 87, 115, 119, 131, 143, 157, 163, 177, 187, 189, 191, 201

Saffron - 199

Smoked Paprika - 113, 131, 199, 205

Truffle Salt - 161

Turmeric - 201

White Pepper - 89

Whole Black Peppercorns - 141

Yellow Curry Powder - 163, 201

VEGETABLES

Arugula - 143, 181, 195, 205

Asparagus - 129, 181, 203

Baby Spinach - 81, 131, 173

Beets - 93, 185

Brussels Sprouts - 151

Butternut Squash - 131, 173

Carrot - 135, 139, 157, 185, 207

Cauliflower - 139, 163, 207

Cherry Tomatoes - 199

English Cucumbers - 153

Fennel - 171, 183, 205

French Green Beans - 135

Garlic - 81, 115, 119, 121, 129, 131, 133, 135, 139, 143, 147, 151, 157, 163, 165, 167, 171, 175, 177, 181, 183, 185, 187, 189, 191, 195, 197, 199, 201, 203, 205, 207

Golden Pearl Onions - 149

Graffiti Eggplant - 199, 205

Grape Tomatoes - 181

Heirloom Tomatoes - 127

Leeks - 135, 173, 181

Orange Pepper - 199, 205

Parsnip - 157, 171

Persian Cucumber - 107, 123

Purple Potatoes - 135, 167

Red Cabbage - 147

Red Onion - 129, 151, 177, 187, 191, 199, 201, 205

Red Pepper - 131, 183, 201

Roma Tomatoes - 135, 161

Shallot - 81, 121, 157, 163, 183, 185, 195, 197

Spring Mix Greens - 137, 141, 179

Sweet Corn - 135, 155, 207

Sweet Potato - 121, 165, 167, 201

Yellow Onion - 131, 139, 171, 175, 193

Yellow Pepper - 199, 205

Yukon Gold Potato - 167, 197

Zucchini - 167

HOW TO USE THIS BOOK

Kitchen Equipment
SIMPLE KITCHEN TOOLS TO MAKE RECIPES FOR TWO

One of the most common questions readers have for me is about what kind of kitchen equipment I use. I think the underlying question is really whether or not they need a lot of fancy or complicated kitchen gadgets for great home cooking? The answer is, no! Kitchen gadgets sure can be fun (Ryan is an avid collector—the shinier and heavier the better). But, very often the simpler the tools, the easier they are to use (and the more space you have!). It's great to have tools that take care of the grunt work, like an electric mixer or food processor, but what typically matters most with cooking is your technique, and your tools should support you. I wrote this book with a curated collection of kitchen accoutrements in mind that you can use over and over again, to ensure success in all your cooking adventures, and not just for two. My recommendations:

6-inch Chef's Knife - my most-used knife in the kitchen for its versatility and ease of handling

Small Paring Knife - more manageable for smaller cutting or "attention to detail" cutting

Serrated Knife - for slicing bread, tomatoes, and other foods that have a tough skin or crust

Honing Steel - to keep your knives as sharp as possible, to be used each time before you begin cutting

Pepper Grinder (adjustable) - freshly cracked pepper is always best, this allows for fine to very course

Rasp - fresh zest is always better, this is a fabulous tool for any citrus for both savory and sweet recipes

Stand Mixer - allows for both hands to be free, and to handle the grunt work of mixing or whipping

Mini Food Processor - wonderful for grinding Parmesan cheese, nuts, pureeing soups, etc.

Sauté Pan (10-inch) - a versatile size with ample cooking surface to brown and sauté

Cast Iron Skillet (8-inch) - perfect for rustic cooking and serving hors d'oeuvre, sides, mains, and desserts

Dutch Oven (3½-quart, with lid) - incredibly versatile and fabulous for soups, stews, and sauces

Small Sauce Pan - for re-heating, melting butter, and versatile everyday use

Medium Sauce Pan - a universal size to cook pasta, soups, lentils, and other legumes

Half Sheet Pan - for roasting vegetables, baking free-form tarts, and an oven-proof tray for nearly anything

Parchment Paper - oven-proof and non-stick liner (easy cleanup) for half sheet pans and other dishes

Baking Dish (1½-quart) - perfectly sized to prepare a multitude of recipes for 2 people

Gratin Dishes (6-7-ounces, 2) - the perfect size to prepare individual servings, both savory and sweet

Ramekins (4-5-ounces, 2) - I love these for serving dips, spreads, and for desserts

Liquid Measuring Cup - glass Pyrex in multiple sizes making measuring liquids a breeze

Dry Measuring Cups (assorted sizes ¼-cup to 1-cup) - for measuring dry ingredients

Measuring Spoons (assorted sizes ⅛-teaspoon to 1-tablespoon) - perfect for portioning salt, pepper, herbs, etc.

Glass Nesting Bowls (graduated sizes, small to very large) - mixing, stirring, prep, storage, etc.

Box Grater - to freshly grate cheeses, vegetables, and even fruits

Pastry Brush - makes buttering a baking pan so simple and fast

French-Style Rolling Pin - tapered ends make it easier to roll out all types of dough and control thickness

Fine Mesh Sieve - for draining, sifting, and straining

ENTERTAINING FOR TWO

Entertaining for Two
STYLES AND MENUS FOR ENTERTAINING AT HOME

Entertaining just for two offers a fabulous spectrum of possibilities! Take full advantage of the different types of spaces available in your home for you and your +1. In this section, I help you get started by laying out five different entertaining vignettes, with entertaining advice and menu options for each, created specifically just for two. Use this section for inspiration and new ideas that you can adapt and incorporate into your own style and aesthetic.

COFFEE TABLE
Cocktails and nibbles

KITCHEN ISLAND
Cooking and entertaining together

DINING TABLE
An updated classic

IN BED
In-bed fête

TV TRAYS
Not your average TV dinner

Coffee Table
COCKTAILS AND NIBBLES

Coffee table entertaining is something I have been doing for years, and you probably have been too, but maybe just never realized it! Think about it, whenever we have people over, we set out a few nibbles, typically on a coffee table, so that our guests can sit, relax, sip a drink, and get caught up with one another. We lay out cocktail napkins, place a vase of flowers, light candles, and so on. Now, if we just go about it in a new and more thought-out way, you can have an entire dinner party around your coffee table! This is especially useful when the space you call home doesn't have a dining room or even a dining table.

I remember one of the apartments I had in Boston was in a vintage building and the space was so small that I kept some of my pantry items in a living room cabinet that also housed books and magazines – yikes! But that never stopped me from having friends over for drinks and nibbles! It was typically a Sunday night, as that was the night *Sex and the City* would air, and I would make Cosmopolitans by the pitcher, lay out cheeses, crackers, and baby dill pickles (I hadn't discovered cornichons yet!), and we would all gather around my coffee table – it was an old uneven trunk – and gossip, laugh, and have a really good time!

I love entertaining around a coffee table so much, that Ryan and I have arranged our main living space to be able to accommodate two sitting areas, each with a coffee table for entertaining! Whether I have over-extended the amount of people our apartment can accommodate (yes, I do this all the time!), or I just want to entertain a friend and change things up, a coffee table acts as not only a place for overflow during a holiday party (like a New Year's Eve dinner we hosted and ended up setting both coffee tables with full dinner place settings and extra floor cushions!), but also a fabulous cozy spot for me and my +1 to sit, gossip, laugh, and have a really good time, still!

The Coffee Table Cocktail Party
I love setting up my coffee table for a cocktail party, for two! I lay out a majority of the things I need ahead of time, and then when my guest arrives all I have to do is make a cocktail, pour wine, or open Champagne and the party begins! When it comes to a coffee table cocktail party, here are a few things I find really make all the difference for preparation and the flow of the party:

① Organize a "bar" on a large tray so that you have everything you need at the ready and you don't have to keep jumping up every time you need a new glass to try a different cocktail. That means extra glasses, different liqueurs and spirts, mixers, sparkling water, and even cocktail straws.

② Have an ice bucket filled with fresh ice and either a small scoop or even thongs. I like to place it onto a small cloth napkin so as the bucket sweats it won't affect the tabletop.

③ Fun paper cocktail napkins are great for hosting any party, and everyday entertaining, really. I also keep a selection on hand for other celebratory occasions like holidays, birthdays, and other themes. Paper cocktail napkins really do add a punch of style and even whimsy!

④ Keep everything low; flowers, un-scented candles, serving pieces, etc. I like to keep everything arranged around the outer perimeter of the coffee to create a "wall of hospitality." Doing this will allow the center of the table to be used as the actual tabletop, without having to reach over or around "this" to get "that."

⑤ Sticky notes are your best friend when you are entertaining! When you are setting up a small space, like a coffee table, mark each serving dish with a sticky note to lay everything out. This will allow you to get a good sense of how your setting looks and flows, but also if it is too tight or cumbersome.

⑥ Keep the menu simple and choose items that can all be served at the same time (and that do not require fussing over) so that you can enjoy the party, too!

The Coffee Table Dinner Party
These are especially fun when your +1 is expecting a "traditional" setting for a soirée, and you surprise them instead with dinner in the living room - game changer! With a few small details it is amazing how fabulous a setting you can create on a coffee table that will impress even the most sophisticated guest:

① Just as you would set a traditional dining table, do the same using everything you would normally use: Tablecloth (or place mats), stemware, flatware, dinnerware, candles, flowers, etc. This applies to a get-together any time of day – remember, a tabletop is a tabletop, so don't let this hinder how simple or elaborate you want to make it!

② Similar to a "wall of hospitality" for a coffee table cocktail party, do the same here and create the perimeter as your "centerpiece." Use different heights of un-scented candles, multiple sizes and variations of flowers and vases, and your beverage of choice nestled into the "centerpiece."

③ If you want to serve hors d'oeuvre or nibbles, have them organized on a tray on a side table or other surface so as not to interfere with the place settings on the coffee table.

④ Designing place settings for two allows you to mix and match pieces! I love collecting antique plates, glassware, and flatware. This is the perfect opportunity to showcase certain collections you have with fewer settings that you may not be able to use if you were entertaining a larger group.

⑤ The menu can really make or break a soirée like this, so be careful! Choose a menu that is easy to eat (this isn't the place to serve piping hot noodles that are already tricky to eat!). Try serving soup in large mugs so that you and your guest can sit back and sip and relax. Serve the entrée and sides pre-plated so that you don't have extra clutter from pans and serving dishes crowding the table. I will say that pre-platting for two people is actually do-able and doesn't require the counter space it does for ten!

ENTERTAINING FOR TWO

Coffee Table
MENUS

Planning a fabulous menu is more than just having a certain number of things that all pair well together. It also has so much to do with texture, color, and how much time everything will take to prepare – I never want to be chained to my kitchen prepping for a party! For a cocktail party at the coffee table, I usually like to serve 2-3 savory options, and 1 sweet option. For a dinner party at the coffee table, I prefer dishes that are easy to maneuver. I accompany both styles of entertaining with cocktails, my *Classic Champagne Elixirs* bar, or a wine selection.

COCKTAIL MENU ONE
Cocktail
Classic Champagne Elixirs, 95

Hors d'Oeuvre
Herbes de Provence Popcorn, 103

Triple Cream Sweet Potato Wedges, 165

Pea & Lemon Tartine, 107

Dessert
Maple & Orange Madeleines, 219

COCKTAIL MENU TWO
Cocktail
Amaretto Sour Martini, 85

Hors d'Oeuvre
Beet & Parsley Canapés, 93

Dried Mango with Whipped Avocado, 97

Yogurt, Fresh Herb & Cucumber Dip, 123

Dessert
Chewy Coconut Cookies, 213

COCKTAIL MENU THREE
Cocktail
Rosé Sangria with Peaches & Rosemary, 109

Hors d'Oeuvre
Baguette Pizza Bites, 87

Spiced Chickpeas, 113

Fried Blue Cheese Olives, 101

Dessert
Shortbread Truffles, 225

GOOD MORNING MENU
Beverage
Lavender Earl Grey Tea, 79

Side
Easy Strawberry Muffins, 73

Salad
French Bistro Vinaigrette, 133

Main Course
Baked Eggs with Goat Cheese, 63

Dessert
Peach & Plum Crisp (optional)*,* 221

DINNER MENU ONE
Cocktail
St-Germain Margarita, 117

Hors d'Oeuvre
Salt & Pepper Potato Chips with Blue Cheese, 111

Salad
Artichoke & Tomato Salad, 127

Side
Balsamic Roasted Pearl Onions, 149

Main Course
Vegetable & Arugula Tacos, 205

Dessert
Drunken Pineapple with Sweet Cream, 217

DINNER MENU TWO
Cocktail
Cabernet Sauvignon

Hors d'Oeuvre
Homemade Ricotta, 105

Soup
Lentil Stew, 135

Side
Herbes de Provence Tomatoes, 161

Main Course
Chicago Sliders, 177

Dessert
Sparkling Raspberry Sorbet, 227

ENTERTAINING FOR TWO

Kitchen Island
COOKING AND ENTERTAINING TOGETHER

The kitchen island, for me, is where I began entertaining Ryan in Seattle when we first started dating. He lived in a gorgeous loft and had a truly fabulous chef's kitchen with a big center island that played a huge role in not only the way we lived, but also ate, entertained, and ultimately wooed one another! We would cook casual meals together, both taking turns stirring the pot (literally!), nibbling on cheeses, sipping fabulous wine, and chatting about the day we both had.

We also have an immense love for ultra-chic hotel bars! We love sitting at the bar for drinks and food, and the little "ceremony" we get to enjoy when the bartender places white napkins on the diagonal and then complete place settings. We often have dinner at the bar instead of sitting at a table. Perhaps it is because our glasses get refilled faster (ha!), or maybe it is because even in the fanciest of restaurants sitting at the bar keeps things casual and more relaxed in some way. Time moves differently at the bar. There aren't the standard cues by a waiter, moving you through courses, asking if you want one last refill. Time slows down at the bar and you enjoy it at a different more casual pace.

That sensation of being less formal and more relaxed is exactly why I love kitchen island entertaining! When two people come together to share a meal at a kitchen island, the mood is relaxed, low-key, and most importantly, interactive. When you sit at a chic bar in a hotel or restaurant, you get to watch the bartender practice their trade – as if having a personal window to the bustle of a chic kitchen. At the same time, you are sitting right next to your +1 and can enjoy their company very personally.

At home, welcoming your +1 with an hors d'oeuvre and cocktail is the way to kick things off to a great start! Then, make the rest of the evening an "event" for you both. Your kitchen island, like sitting at a bar, weaves your +1 into seeing what's happening in the kitchen and being able to share in it all. Cook together, entertain each other, and most importantly, laugh together!

Entertaining around your kitchen island can be très chic, but also feel casual and effortless. These are some of my favorite ways to zhush what is perhaps the most under-utilized surface for a kitchen soirée for two:

① Just like in hotel bars, use napkins as place mats! Lay them out on the diagonal and then build your place settings from there.

② Use fresh herbs instead of flowers. You can use them while you cook and also garnish your finished dishes. This is always an unexpected surprise!

③ Take it one step further and make other ingredients part of your table setting. Bowls of lemons that will be juiced and zested, vegetables that will be chopped as part of a recipe, and wine that you can cook with and drink!

④ If you have fine China, silver, and crystal – please use it, all! It isn't serving any purpose sitting behind glass or in a drawer. While I recognize that handwashing such things is time consuming, then a setting for two people is the perfect time to use your best pieces as clean-up goes rather quickly just for two. It also creates a high/low thing that connects to the idea of casual, yet chic – sitting at a kitchen island eating off fine China, especially when you serve something rustic, like my *Caramelized Onion & White Cheddar Mac 'n Cheese* (page 175).

⑤ Have a game of checkers set up or a dice game ready to go! This is especially fun to just sip wine and enjoy nibbles before (or while) you are cooking. But perhaps stay away from anything that requires major concentration, like Operation!

⑥ A kitchen island is also a great canvas to host a cocktail party for two with lots of smaller bites, nibbles, and boozy offerings! Refer to page 39 for some ideas on hosting a fabulous cocktail party.

⑦ In this case, timing is not everything! Like when sitting at a bar, let time move differently. Don't worry about serving everything all at the same time. Serve each side as they are done, almost like tapas-style, and serve the main course with a big green salad.

⑧ Serve right from the pan. Don't bother transferring finished recipes to serving pieces. Take advantage of the space and being right in the kitchen!

⑨ The same goes for dessert! Choose something that can be prepared quickly, like my *Petit S'mores Croissants* (page 223), and that can be assembled with the help or involvement of your +1, then bake them off when you are ready for the dessert course. I have a number of desserts that are kitchen-friendly experiences to share with your +1: *Warm Chocolate Pots with Grand Marnier & Cherries* (page 231), rolling my *Shortbread Truffles* (page 225), and churning the base for my *Brown Sugar Ice Cream* (page 211). All of these desserts take hardly any time to assemble, prepare, or bake.

⑩ Last, but certainly not least, take full advantage of the easy and elegant environment of your kitchen island, and have fun! Have fun with your setting, have fun with your menu, and enjoy letting time move at a different pace for some fun with your +1!

ENTERTAINING FOR TWO

Kitchen Island
MENUS

GOOD MORNING MENU
Beverage
French Roast Coffee with Cream and Sugar

Freshly-Squeezed Orange Juice

Side
Berry & Basil Compote, 67

Earl Grey & Lemon Butter, 71

Toast Basket

Main Course
Banana & Maple Dutch-Flan, 65

MENU TWO
Cocktail
French Basil 75, 91

Hors d'Oeuvre
Spicy Garlic Edamame, 115

Soup
Butternut Squash & Black Bean Soup, 131

Side
Carpaccio of Cucumber, 153

Roasted Cauliflower with Curried Brown Butter, 163

Dessert
Chewy Coconut Cookies, 213

MENU THREE
Cocktail
Dry Rosé Wine

Hors d'Oeuvre
Salted Cashews

Fig & Goat Cheese Truffles, 99

Salad
Matchstick Apple Salad, 137

Main Course
Fennel & Red Pepper Risotto, 183

Dessert
Store-Bought Cake Made Fabulous!, 229

MENU FOUR
Cocktail
Amaretto Sour Martini, 85

Hors d'Oeuvre
Sweet Potato & Triple Cream Brie Tartine, 121

Spiced Chickpeas, 113

Salad
Roasted Fruit with Rosemary Vinaigrette, 141

Side
Corn Gratin with White Cheddar, 155

Dessert
Drunken Pineapple with Sweet Cream, 217

MENU FIVE
Cocktail
Champagne

Hors d'Oeuvre
Baked Camembert with Pears & Maple, 89

Main Course
Country Frittata with Petite Salad, 181

Dessert
Crème Brûlée with Honey & Lemon, 215

MENU SIX
Cocktail
Crisp White Wine

Hors d'Oeuvre
Sun Dried Tomato & White Bean Dip, 119

Soup
Asparagus Soup, 129

Side
Dried Figs & Warm Orzo, 159

Main Course
Pear & Onion Tart, 193

Dessert
Fresh Berries with Whipped Cream, 229

Dining Table
AN UPDATED CLASSIC

Perhaps the most common surface we all think of when it comes to hosting a meal at home is the dining room table. Whether it is round, square, oval, or rectangle, a dining table is the place for people to gather, share a meal, and solve the world's problems (after a few bottles of wine!). Setting a large table for four, six, or eight people is easy and really doesn't require too much thinking when it comes to the proper placement of each place setting, flowers, candles, and even the actual dishes each recipe is served in. Really, the formula for setting a dining table has been set for centuries!

For two people, you and your +1, how do you prevent a large table from feeling cold and not intimate? A long table has so often been portrayed, both in movies and commercials, with each person sitting at opposite ends comically screaming at one another to, "Pass the salt!" Well, now you can save your voice, have your salt (and pepper!), and enjoy the company you have invited to be with you without screaming, dahling! The time of day you decide to entertaining will dictate what type of accoutrements are needed for your menu, regardless of how simple or elaborate. Use my ideas here for setting a table for two, with a welcomed twist!

It isn't about setting the "perfect" table – there isn't any such thing! A table should reflect your personal style, tastes, and use what you have, perhaps layered differently each time, to help give your collections a new and revitalized breath of fresh air:

1. I prefer to use the end of a table (if the shape is appropriate) that looks back into the space you are entertaining in.

2. Sitting directly next to your +1 (instead of across) immediately makes everything feel much more relaxed and less formal. It also allows you to interact with one another more naturally.

3. I love mixing earthy textures like woven placemats and un-ironed linen napkins with sterling silver-rimmed stemware (I love the way it looks when it is slightly tarnished), crystal candle sticks, classic white plates, printed salad plates, and footed lion-head soup bowls. The footed soup bowls add height to what can end up being a very flat setting.

4. Flowers, flowers, and more flowers! And not from a florist, but rather from my favorite grocery store or farmers market. I typically choose either a single color palette and buy three to five different varieties in that color, or color-block different varieties. Either way you choose, try arranging them in different-sized vessels, all with different heights.

ENTERTAINING FOR TWO

⑤ I have always said that a flower arrangement on a table should never be over eight inches tall, as you want to make sure people can converse easily with one another and not "peer through a forest" trying to have a conversation. For your Dining Table for two, throw that rule out the window! Here, you want to make a large table feel intimate. The easiest way to do that is by having taller arrangements, candle sticks with un-scented candles, and even your wine and sparkling water bottles help create a hard-stop visually for where you want the table to begin and end. My table is 118-inches long, but in the opposite photograph, I have created a table that is visually one-third the size. This instantly makes the setting cozier and inviting. If you have a round or square table, you can adopt the same idea and technique of creating a visual hard-stop, you may have to switch things around a bit to get the proportions right.

⑥ Lay out your place settings and then take a seat (literally!) to place your flowers, candles, etc. around the table until it feels comfortable, but not over crowded or tight. Having a seated view is dramatically different than standing over a table to create the setting. Remember, we're used to the pattern and repetition in places settings for a standard seating and you're trying to create a more intimate space.

⑦ If you have fine China, silver, and crystal – please use it, all! Just as I mentioned in the Kitchen Island segment (page 43), it isn't serving any purpose sitting behind glass or in a drawer. While I recognize that handwashing such things is time consuming, a setting for two people does go rather quickly when it comes time to clean up.

⑧ I am a firm believer in making sure everyone is having fun! After all, the art of in-home dining and entertaining is back, and here to stay! We must always strive to eat well, laugh often, and share the love as much as we can! And hey, raise our glasses to never take for granted this thing we call life – zivio!

ENTERTAINING FOR TWO

Dining Table
MENUS

GOOD MORNING MENU
Beverage
Lavender Earl Grey Tea, 79

Pineapple Juice

Side
Easy Strawberry Muffins, 73

Main Course
Savory Dutch-Flan with Golden Potatoes, 197

Dessert
Shortbread Truffles, 225

MENU TWO
Cocktail
Barolo

Hors d'Oeuvre
Fig & Goat Cheese Truffles, 99

Soup
Asparagus Soup, 129

Salad
Artichoke & Tomato Salad, 127

Side
Balsamic Roasted Pearl Onions, 149

Main Course
Herbed Cannellini Bean "Meatballs", 187

Dessert
Peach & Plum Crisp, 221

MENU THREE
Cocktail
Classic Champagne Elixirs, 95

Hors d'Oeuvre
Salted Marcona Almonds

Salad
French Bistro Vinaigrette, 133

Main Course
Stove-Top Paella, 199

Dessert
Sparkling Raspberry Sorbet, 227

MENU FOUR
Cocktail
Dry French Rosé

Hors d'Oeuvre
Herbes de Provence Popcorn, 103

Soup
Lentil Stew, 135

Main Course
Country Frittata with Petite Salad, 181

Dessert
Crème Brûlée with Honey & Lemon, 215

MENU FIVE
Cocktail
Amaretto Sour Martini, 85

Hors d'Oeuvre
Dried Mango with Whipped Avocado, 97

Spiced Chickpeas, 113

Main Course
Vietnamese-Inspired Pho, 207

Dessert
Chewy Coconut Cookies, 213

MENU SIX
Cocktail
Crisp White Wine

Hors d'Oeuvre
Fried Blue Cheese Olives, 101

Salad
Matchstick Apple Salad, 137

Main Course
Truffled Toast with Asparagus, 203

Dessert
Warm Chocolate Pots with Grand Marnier & Cherries, 231

In Bed
IN-BED FÊTE

Growing up, there were TV events like the annual broadcasts of *The Wizard of Oz*, *The Great Pumpkin*, classic Christmas cartoons, and other iconic movies that were a cause of planning and preparing so they could be enjoyed thoroughly! On those nights my cousins and I would all be at our nan's house, where she would pull out the sofa bed in the living room, make giant bowls of popcorn, and we would all pile onto the bed and watch whatever was on that night – these memories are some of what I treasure most!

Of course, the adults would all be in the kitchen playing gin rummy, drinking pink Chablis (nan's favorite!), and literally laughing so loud (the wine, perhaps?!) that we would need to turn up the television! Not much has changed for me for the when having a fun in-bed fête. I lived in NYC for years with roommates, and your bed becomes an all-purpose spot in your apartment. I had a circular wooden board, about 42-inches round, covered with a wipe-able material, that I stored under my bed and would literally pull out every day and use as a tabletop to eat take-out, pay bills, and where friends would rest their Champagne glasses while I asked their opinion on my outfit (again!) before heading out for a night on the town!

The bed is also the place where you tend to a friend with a cold, have pillow talk with your partner, have a pajama party with your best friend watching fashion documentaries (or reality TV!), flip through books and magazines, and indulge in fattening food (Champagne and French fries, anyone?!). It doesn't matter the scale of your living space, but rather how you use it in its entirely. Think about your bedroom as a weekday treat, or a weekend re-treat.

It doesn't take a lot of time to plan a fun (the most important element!) in-bed fête! It doesn't require multiple courses, place settings, or even a lot of cooking. It does however require you to think outside the box and be creative with your planning:

① Just like planning a dinner party, start with why you want to plan an in-bed fête. BFF night, re-runs of *I Love Lucy* to cheer someone up, or a romantic breakfast in bed. The "why" will immediately dictate how you proceed with the menu, atmosphere, and other details.

② No formalities allowed! Casual is key, and a welcomed breath of fresh air, especially considering the location!

③ Keep the theme light-hearted and fun. Celebrate a friend's birthday (they will never forget this one!), or cheer someone up and show up ready to have a great time and laugh, or just relax and unwind.

④ Have an extra pair of new satin pajamas ready for your +1 for a little more fun! They also make for a wonderful gift!

ENTERTAINING FOR TWO

⑤ Choose a theme and color and run with it! Have fun creating an atmosphere and setting. Hot-pink color scheme (*What A Way To Go*, anyone!?), or all-white for a hotel or spa-like effect, or go with your +1's favorite color or favorite travel destination and customize the theme for them. The scale is so much easier to manage as you're enjoying all of this from bed, and not having to decorate the entire house.

⑥ Instead of serving multiple courses, choose small bites and nibbles to start. Things like my *Herbes de Provence Popcorn* (page 103), and *Fried Blue Cheese Olives* (page 101). Choose recipes that are easy to serve and do not require being serving in a hot pan or dish. This isn't the place to balance a fondue set with flaming sterno pots!

⑦ A breakfast tray is a very handy thing to have on hand. I use mine rather like a side table to hold nibbles, wine, and flowers.

⑧ Serve one main dish, like my *Hot & Sour Coconut Noodles* (page 189), or my *Orange & Rosemary Cream Sauce* (page 191), and serve them in over-sized bowls. This makes for easy eating and you both can sit back and enjoy.

⑨ Dessert should also be easy and elegant, and a course that doesn't require a lot of fussing around. Even a glass of red wine with different chocolate bars would be fabulous. Candy always wins!

⑩ Don't feel like the entire get together has to happen only on the bed. Perhaps have dessert and Champagne in bed to finish out a dinner and watch your favorite movie, have at-home spa night, or just stay up late and talk shit (or spill the T!).

ENTERTAINING FOR TWO

In Bed
MENUS

MENU ONE
Cocktail
Basil French 75, 91

Hors d'Oeuvre
Beet & Parsley Canapés, 93

Side
Dried Figs & Warm Orzo, 159

Main Course
Chicago Sliders, 177

Dessert
Brown Sugar Ice Cream, 211

MENU TWO
Cocktail
Amaretto Sour Martini, 85

Hors d'Oeuvre
Gruyère Cheese & Fig Preserves on Black Pepper Water Crackers

Soup
Roasted Cauliflower Soup, 139

Main Course
French Lentils with Apples & Beets, 185

Dessert
Shortbread Truffles, 225

MENU THREE
Cocktail
Dry French Rosé

Hors d'Oeuvre
Herbes de Provence Popcorn, 103

Fried Blue Cheese Olives, 101

Fig & Goat Cheese Truffles, 99

Dessert
Petit S'mores Croissants, 223

MENU FOUR
Cocktail
St-Germain Margarita, 117

Hors d'Oeuvre
Spicy Garlic Edamame, 115

Main Course
Hot & Sour Coconut Noodles, 189

Dessert
Chewy Coconut Cookies, 213

MENU FIVE
Cocktail
Côtes du Rhône

Hors d'Oeuvre
Salt & Pepper Potato Chips

Main Course
Sweet Potato Curry, 201

Dessert
Drunken Pineapple with Sweet Cream, 217

MENU SIX
Cocktail
Classic Champagne Elixirs, 95

Dessert
Store-Bought Cake Made Fabulous!, 229

Dessert
Brown Sugar Ice Cream, 211

ENTERTAINING FOR TWO

TV Trays
NOT YOUR AVERAGE TV DINNER

When I first mentioned to friends that I was going to include a section in this book dedicated to TV tray entertaining, they thought I had either too much Champagne, or I had fallen on my head (or both!). I actually have fond memories of my great-grandmother and grammy sitting in front of little rickety TV trays in the evenings, with bowls of vanilla ice cream, watching *Happy Days*, *All In The Family*, and even re-runs of *The Three Stooges* (my great-grandmother's favorite!).

Their trays were made on very thin aluminum, and the kind that if you just walked by, making the tiniest bit of a breeze, they would immediately collapse to the floor in a crash! Or, your feet would get all tangled in the legs and down they went. I swear, this must have happened daily. Yet, I always got a hard candy from the top shelf in the coat closet and a dollar bill from the pocket of my great-grandmother's house coat. So, I guess I didn't annoy them too badly!

When Ryan and I first moved to Chicago from Seattle, we arrived way before our household did. We had nothing but a picnic basket, laptops, a printer, and some clothes! Luckily, the picnic basket had place settings for two (complete with cloth napkins and a wine opener!). We had a hardware store only a short walk away and one day I came home with TV trays. Ryan looked at me for a split second, and then said, "Darling, if anyone can make TV trays chic, it is you!"

So, that is exactly what I did, for two months! While we waited for our moving truck (we may have given ourselves a little *too* much time to drive across the country and get ourselves set up in Chicago), we "roughed" it each night without a dining table. Instead, we had really good food, sitting on a sofa our neighbors lent us (even with *zero* furniture, we still invited people over to introduce ourselves and have a nibble!), using the TV trays I set up with proper place settings, and enjoyed just being in love. To this day, we always re-create the first meal I cooked and served the night I brought home TV trays: A bottle of Champagne, my *Herbed Cannellini "Meatballs"* (page 187), *Spicy Oregano Sauce* (from *Entertaining with Love*), and lots of really good Belgian milk chocolate!

Just like the idea of an in-bed fête, a TV tray soirée is an unexpected and welcomed surprise to shake-up entertaining at home:

1. To cover or not to cover?! I like to use French tea towels (or vintage tea towels) as a covering. I have a drawer filled with tea towels of different colors and patterns that I use not only for this purpose, but they also make fabulous over-sized napkins.

ENTERTAINING FOR TWO

② Use individual candle lamps to add a bit of glamour. These remind me of something you would see in a nightclub or café in the 1930s.

③ Small bud vases work best if you want to add blooms to your trays. You can also use juice glasses or even aperitif glasses for vases.

④ Stick with stemless glassware for all beverages. This will help you and your +1 to avoid things toppling over and wasting wine – a travesty!

⑤ If you have a coffee table, use it to your advantage and stage things you would normally have on a dining table like wine, side dishes, and even the next course, or dessert. This will allow you to sit and enjoy without shifting your tray to run to the kitchen for the next course, or something you forgot.

⑥ Make eating on TV trays feel nostalgic by serving each course covered in aluminum foil. Think how happily surprised your +1 will be when you peel off the foil and reveal a delicious dish like my *Fennel & Red Pepper Risotto* (page 183), instead of gloopy mashed potatoes and lumpy gravy – ick!

⑦ After you have finished eating, clear off the coffee table, set out a *Classic Champagne Elixirs* bar (page 95), and play cards! There is no need to re-locate the party when everything you need is at your fingertips!

⑧ I've also used TV trays as extra tables during larger cocktail parties (covered in to-the-floor cloths) to provide another surface for food, a wine bar, or even as a collection point for used glassware. They can also be nestled by the dining table to be used to stage dessert and cheeses. Since they fold up flat, you can store them just about anywhere.

ENTERTAINING FOR TWO

TV Trays
MENUS

GOOD MORNING MENU
Beverage
Freshly Squeezed Orange Juice

Side
Homemade Granola, 77

Fig & Cream Scones, 75

Main Course
Cinnamon Raisin French Toast with Apples & Mascarpone, 69

MENU TWO
Cocktail
Rosé Sangria with Peaches & Rosemary, 109

Hors d'Oeuvre
Homemade Ricotta, 105

Salad
French Bistro Vinaigrette, 133

Soup
Lentil Stew, 135

Side
Brussels Sprouts with Strawberries, 151

Dessert
Crème Brûlée with Honey & Lemon, 215

MENU THREE
Cocktail
Stella Artois

Hors d'Oeuvre
Spicy Garlic Edamame, 115

Side
Apple & Blue Cheese Slaw, 147

Main Course
Chicago Sliders, 177

Dessert
Peach & Plum Crisp, 221

MENU FOUR
Cocktail
Basil French 75, 91

Hors d'Oeuvre
Pea & Lemon Tartine, 107

Soup
Asparagus Soup, 129

Main Course
Cinnamon Raisin Grilled Cheese, 179

Dessert
Maple & Orange Madeleines, 219

MENU FIVE
Cocktail
Dry White Wine

Hors d'Oeuvre
Yogurt, Fresh Herb & Cucumber Dip, 123

Side
Triple Cream Sweet Potato Wedges, 165

Roasted Cauliflower with Curried Browned Butter, 163

Dessert
Drunken Pineapple with Sweet Cream, 217

MENU SIX
Cocktail
Amaretto Sour Martini, 85

Hors d'Oeuvre
Baguette Pizza Bites, 87

Salad
Warm White Bean Salad, 143

Side
Corn Gratin with White Cheddar, 155

Dessert
Brown Sugar Ice Cream, 211

EARLYBIRDS & BOOKWORMS
TUESDAY, SEPTEMBER 18, 2018

ROASTED RED PEPPER, SPINACH & GRUYERE QUICHE

POTATO CAKE

FRESH FRUIT

***

OUR GRATITUDE
TO THE HOST COMMITTEE
FOR SUPPORTING TODAY'S EVENT

MELISSA BABCOCK
SHERRILL BODINE
PAULA BORG
TRUDY CASSIN
CHERYL COLEMAN
SUSAN GOHL
SHERRY LEA HOLSON
MARCI HOLZER
RON KATZ
MARY LASKY
SALLY JO MORRIS
MARK OLLEY
VONITA REESCER
SUSAN REGENSTEIN
MYRA REILLY
MAMIE WALTON

RECIPES FOR TWO

Recipes for Two
EASY AND ELEGANT VEGETARIAN COOKING

"You don't have to cook fancy or complicated masterpieces - just good food from fresh ingredients."
—Julia Child

Those words capture so well my philosophy for cooking in general, and my approach to creating the recipes for Table for Two. Giving your undivided attention to your +1 is at the heart of the experience I aimed to capture with this book. The food you prepare should be to support that and doesn't need to be complicated, fussy, or overly-extravagant. This section is filled with my vegetarian recipes perfectly portioned for two, with fresh ingredients, straight-forward preparation, and truly fabulous flavors.

GOOD MORNING
Delicious recipes for a simple and chic breakfast or brunch

HORS D'OEUVRE & COCKTAILS
Cocktails and nibbles perfected for two

SOUPS & SALADS
Fresh and flavorful first courses

SIDES
Fabulous dishes to compliment any menu

MAIN COURSES
Perfectly portioned for you and your +1

DESSERTS
The perfect ending for any occasion

GOOD MORNING

Good Morning
DELICIOUS RECIPES FOR A SIMPLE AND CHIC BREAKFAST OR BRUNCH

Baked Eggs with Goat Cheese, 63

Banana & Maple Dutch-Flan, 65

Berry & Basil Compote, 67

Cinnamon Raisin French Toast with Apples & Mascarpone, 69

Earl Grey & Lemon Butter, 71

Easy Strawberry Muffins, 73

Fig & Cream Scones, 75

Homemade Granola, 77

Lavender Earl Grey Tea, 79

Stuffed Croissants with Spinach, 81

GOOD MORNING

Baked Eggs *with* Goat Cheese

A DELICIOUSLY VERSATILE DISH FOR BREAKFAST, BRUNCH, LUNCH, OR EVEN DINNER!

DIRECTIONS

1. Pre-heat the oven to 450 degrees F.

2. Crack 2 eggs each into two small bowls, being careful not to break the yolks. Set aside.

3. Place 2 individual round gratin dishes (6 to 7-inch diameter) onto a sheet pan. Add 1 tablespoon of both cream and butter to each dish. Place in the pre-heated oven for 3 minutes.

4. Remove the sheet pan from the oven. Moving quickly and carefully, slide the cracked eggs into each gratin dish, being careful not to break the yolks. Top each one evenly with the roasted red peppers, Gournay (Boursin®) cheese, salt, and pepper.

5. Return the sheet pan to the oven and bake for 7-8 minutes, until the egg whites are just set.

6. Remove from the oven and sprinkle with fresh parsley and Parmesan cheese.

7. Allow to rest for 2 minutes before serving.

INGREDIENTS & PREP

Eggs - 4 extra-large, at room temperature

Heavy Cream - 2 tablespoons

Butter - 2 tablespoons, unsalted, at room temperature

Gournay Cheese - 2 tablespoons, crumbled (Boursin® Garlic & Fine Herbs recommended)

Roasted Red Peppers - 2 tablespoons, ¼-inch diced

Sea Salt - ½ teaspoon, divided

Black Pepper - ½ teaspoon, freshly cracked, divided

Parsley - 2 tablespoons, fresh, roughly chopped (Italian flat leaf parsley recommended)

Parmesan Cheese - 2 tablespoons, freshly grated (Parmigiano-Reggiano recommended)

PLANNING

Bake - 7-8 minutes, at 450 degrees F

Yield - serves 2

TIP
For this recipe, a 7-inch round gratin dish is the most useful size. It is also useful for other individually proportioned recipes, both savory and sweet. You can find good quality gratin dishes in most cookware shops, online, and even high-end grocery stores.

IDEA
I just adore this recipe—it is both easy and elegant, and can be served any time of the day for a casual or formal occasion. Try serving it with toast points for a breakfast or brunch, or with a petite green salad for a lunch or dinner. To heighten its elegance, a glass of crisp rosé wine or Champagne (regardless the time of day!) will always pair perfectly!

NOTES

GOOD MORNING

Banana & Maple Dutch-Flan

IF A DUTCH BABY AND A FLAN WALKED INTO A BAR... THIS WOULD BE THEIR OVEN CHILD!

DIRECTIONS

1. Pre-heat the oven to 425 degrees F.

2. Place 2 individual round gratin dishes (6 to 7-inch diameter) onto a sheet pan. Place 1 tablespoon of butter into each gratin dish. Set aside.

3. In a glass measuring cup, add the milk, flour, eggs, vanilla, honey, and salt. Whisk until completely smooth.

4. Once the oven is fully pre-heated, place the sheet tray with the gratin dishes into the hot oven for 3 minutes.

5. Next, carefully remove the sheet pan from the oven and immediately pour the batter into the two gratin dishes, evenly dividing the batter – each gratin dish should hold 1 cup of batterr.

6. Return the sheet pan with the gratin dishes to the oven and bake for 14-15 minutes, until the sides are puffed up and golden brown.

7. Remove from the oven, add the sliced bananas, drizzle with maple syrup, dust with powdered sugar, and serve immediately.

INGREDIENTS & PREP

Butter – 2 tablespoons, unsalted, at room temperature

Whole Milk – ¾ cup

Flour – ¾ cup

Eggs – 3 extra-large, lightly beaten, at room temperature

Vanilla – ½ teaspoon, pure extract

Honey – 2 teaspoons

Sea Salt – ¼ teaspoon

Bananas – 2, peeled and thinly sliced

Maple Syrup – ½ cup, Grade A

Powdered Sugar – for garnish

PLANNING

Bake – 14-15 minutes, at 425 degrees F

Yield – serves 2

A LITTLE STORY

When I was in my kitchen testing this recipe, I was aiming for something that was more substantial in texture than a traditional Dutch Baby, as they tend to have a very thin bottom. Instead, I wanted a flan-like texture, but also something more recognizable to be served at breakfast. After adjusting the ratios of flour, eggs, and milk, I was amazed at what came out of the oven—a fuller-bodied and creamier-textured bottom, similar to a flan but still with the light and airy sides of a Dutch Baby. I chose to fill it with sliced bananas and Vermont maple syrup, but this would be equally scrumptious with the filling from my *Cinnamon Raisin French Toast with Apples & Mascarpone* (page 69).

NOTES

GOOD MORNING

Berry & Basil Compote

A SWEET AND SAVOR CONCOCTION THAT IS SURE TO AWAKEN YOUR TASTE BUDS

DIRECTIONS

1. In a medium sauce pan set over medium heat, add all of the ingredients. Bring to just under the boiling point, then reduce the heat to medium-low, and simmer for 25-30 minutes, or until most of the liquid is gone leaving behind a luscious reduction of berries.

2. Pour the mixture into a heat-proof bowl and allow to cool to room temperature. Once cooled, transfer to an air-tight container and store in the refrigerator, for up to 5 days.

Tip: Set a small strainer over a bowl when juicing the orange to catch any excess pulp and seeds.

INGREDIENTS & PREP

Frozen Berry Medley - 1 bag (10 ounces), blueberries, blackberries, strawberries, and raspberries

Basil - 1½ cups leaves, fresh, very finely minced

Sugar - 2 tablespoons

Granny Smith Apple - 1 medium, peeled, cored, ¼-inch diced

Orange - 1 medium, juiced, zested

Sea Salt - ¼ teaspoon

PLANNING

Yield - makes 2 cups

IDEA

I love pairing this sweet and savory compote with waffles, toast, or pancakes for breakfast, or with cheeses and baguette for cocktails!

NOTES

Cinnamon Raisin French Toast *with* Apples & Mascarpone
THIS REMAKE OF CLASSIC FRENCH TOAST IS THE BUSINESS

DIRECTIONS

MASCARPONE CREAM
1. Combine both ingredients in a small bowl. Whisk until completely smooth. Set aside.

WARM APPLE TOPPING
2. In a medium saucepan set over medium heat, add the butter. Once melted and hot, add the apples. Cook for 10 minutes, stirring occasionally, until tender.
3. Next, add the vanilla, honey, maple syrup, salt, nutmeg, cinnamon, orange zest, and raisins. Cook for another 5 minutes, stirring occasionally. Remove from the heat and cover tightly. Set aside.

CUSTARD
4. In a small dish, whisk together the eggs, half & half, orange zest, salt, and vanilla until well mixed.

ASSEMBLY
5. Pre-heat the oven to 200 degrees F.
6. In a medium sauté pan set over medium heat, add 1 tablespoon of butter.
7. Dip three slices of bread into the egg mixture, letting each soak for about 5 seconds on each side. Place each dipped bread slice into the sauté pan and cook for about 5-7 minutes on one side until golden brown, then flip, and cook on the other side for an additional 2-3 minutes.
8. Place the cooked slices onto a sheet pan and transfer into the warm oven. Wipe out the sauté pan with a dry paper towel, and repeat the same process with the remaining 3 slices of bread.
9. Once all 6 slices of bread have been sautéed, transfer 3 slices to each plate. With a spoon, evenly distribute the warm apple mixture over the bread, and then spoon over the mascarpone cream. Serve immediately.

INGREDIENTS & PREP

Cinnamon Raisin Bread – 6 slices

MASCARPONE CREAM
Mascarpone – ¼ cup

Half & Half – 1 tablespoon

WARM APPLE TOPPING
Butter – 3 tablespoons, unsalted, at room temperature

Granny Smith Apple – 1 medium, peeled, cored, ½-inch diced

Vanilla – ½ teaspoon, pure extract

Honey – 1 tablespoon

Maple Syrup – ½ cup, Grade A

Sea Salt – ¼ teaspoon

Nutmeg – ⅛ teaspoon

Cinnamon – ⅛ teaspoon

Orange Zest – 1 teaspoon

Raisins – ⅓ cup

CUSTARD
Eggs – 2 extra-large, at room temperature

Half & Half – ½ cup

Orange Zest – 1 teaspoon

Sea Salt – ¼ teaspoon

Vanilla – ½ teaspoon, pure extract

Butter – 2 tablespoons, unsalted, at room temperature

PLANNING
Pre-Heat Oven – 200 degrees F

Yield – serves 2

GOOD MORNING

Earl Grey & Lemon Butter

A BRIGHT AND ELEGANT COMPOUND BUTTER FOR A SUBTLE TWIST ON CLASSICS

DIRECTIONS

1. Place all the ingredients into a small bowl and mix until combined.
2. Transfer to a serving dish or ramekin. Enjoy at room temperature.

INGREDIENTS & PREP

Butter - 1 stick, unsalted, at room temperature

Earl Grey Tea - 1 tea bag, leaves only (your favorite variety recommended)

Lemon Zest - ½ teaspoon

Honey - 2 teaspoons

Fleur de Sel - ⅛ teaspoon

PLANNING

Yield - 8 tablespoons

TIP

To store the butter, cut a strip of parchment paper 5 inches wide and spoon the mixture evenly across the short end of the paper. Roll the parchment paper over the butter and into a log about 1 inch in diameter. Twist the ends of the parchment paper roll to close. Refrigerate for up to 5 days. Once chilled, you can slice the butter roll into round pads and then allow to come to room temperature before serving.

IDEA

I love using my *Earl Grey & Lemon Butter* on warm biscuits, pancakes, toasted brioche, and on my *Easy Strawberry Muffins* (page 73). For an elegant twist on old classics, you can also use it as a spread for cucumber sandwiches, or as a substitute for plain butter in a shortbread cookie recipe. Just make sure to adjust the salt in an existing recipe as this compound butter already has salt in it.

NOTES

GOOD MORNING

Easy Stawberry Muffins

ONE OF THE SIMPLEST AND YET MOST DELICIOUS TREATS FOR BREAKFAST OR BRUNCH

DIRECTIONS

1. Pre-heat the oven to 375 degrees F. Line a standard muffin tin with 6 paper liners.

2. In a small bowl, combine the diced strawberries, sugar, and lemon zest. Stir and allow to sit for 5 minutes.

3. In a large bowl, sift together the flour, baking powder, baking soda, and salt.

4. Then, add the half & half, egg, and cooled butter to the dry ingredients. With a spatula, stir until just combined (do not over-mix—it will make the muffins dense).

5. Now, gently fold in the strawberries, sugar, and lemon zest, until just combined.

6. Next, using a 2¼-inch scoop, divide the batter evenly among the lined muffin wells.

7. Bake for 20-23 minutes, until the muffin tops are golden brown.

8. Remove the muffin pan from the oven and place on a wire rack. Allow to cool for 15 minutes. Then, remove the muffins from the tin. Serve warm or at room temperature.

Tip: To store or freeze the muffins, ensure they have cooled completely. Whether you are storing the muffins in the freezer, or in an air tight container, you can "revive" them before serving! Cut them in half vertically, spread a bit of butter on each cut side, and place the buttered sides down in a small sauté pan set over medium heat. Toast until golden brown! Serve with more butter or preserves.

To freeze: Wrap each muffin in a double layer of plastic wrap, then place the muffins into a freezer bag and seal tightly with as little air in the bag as possible (without mashing the muffins). The muffins will stay fresh in the freezer for up to 4 weeks. Allow to come to room temperature before serving.

To store: Place the muffins in an air-tight container and store at room temperature. The muffins with remain fresh for up to 3 days.

INGREDIENTS & PREP

Strawberries - ¾ cups, hulled, ½-inch diced

Sugar - ⅓ cup, plus 1 tablespoon

Lemon Zest - 1 teaspoon, freshly zested

Flour - ¾ cup, plus 1 tablespoon

Baking Powder - ¾ teaspoon

Baking Soda - ¼ teaspoon

Sea Salt - ¼ teaspoon

Half & Half - ⅓ cup, at room temperature

Egg - 1 extra-large, lightly beaten, at room temperature

Butter - 5 tablespoons, melted, cooled completely

PLANNING

Bake - 20-23 minutes, at 375 degrees F

Yield - 6 muffins

NOTES

GOOD MORNING

Fig & Cream Scones

FROM HIGH TEA TO THE HEIGHT OF TEA!

DIRECTIONS

1. Pre-heat the oven to 400 degrees F. Line a sheet pan with parchment paper and set aside.

2. In a small bowl, toss the diced figs with 1 tablespoon of flour and set aside.

3. In the bowl of an electric mixer fitted with a paddle attachment, add the remaining 1 cup of flour, as well as the sugar, baking powder, salt, and cold butter. Mix on low speed until the butter is crumbled to the size of peas.

4. With the mixer still running on low speed, add the cold heavy cream, lightly beaten egg, and figs. Mix until just combined. The dough will be very sticky.

5. Place the dough onto a lightly floured surface and gently pat the dough into a disk.

6. Using a well-floured rolling pin, roll the dough into a square, approximately ¾-inch thick. Cut the square in half, then cut each half again on the diagonal to make triangle-shaped scones.

7. Place each scone onto the prepared sheet pan and brush with egg wash. Sprinkle the tops with more sugar, if desired.

8. Bake for 20-22 minutes, until the tops and edges are lightly brown.

9. Remove from the oven, and transfer to a cooling rack to cool fully.

TIP

If you do not have a stand mixer, use a pastry blender to quickly cut the butter into pea-sized pieces in the flour mixture. Then, add the cold cream and lightly beaten egg. With your hand slightly cupped, quickly work the liquid into the flour and butter mixture. Follow the remaining directions as stated above.

INGREDIENTS & PREP

Flour - 1 cup, plus 1 tablespoon, all purpose

Sugar - 2 teaspoons, plus more for garnish

Baking Powder - 1½ teaspoons

Sea Salt - ½ teaspoon

Butter - 6 tablespoons, unsalted, very cold, diced

Eggs - 1 extra-large, lightly beaten, at room temperature

Heavy Cream - ¼ cup, very cold

Dried Figs - ½ cup, diced ½-inch (Black Mission variety preferred)

Egg Wash - 1 extra-large egg lightly beaten with 1 tablespoon of water

PLANNING

Bake - 20-22 minutes, at 400 degrees F

Yield - makes 4 scones

NOTES

GOOD MORNING

Homemade Granola

THE PERFECT TOPPING FOR YOGURT, OR EVEN FROMAGE BLANC FOR A TWIST ON DESSERT

DIRECTIONS

1. Pre-heat the oven to 325 degrees F.

2. In a small bowl, whisk together the honey and canola oil until combined. Set aside.

3. In a large bowl, add the oats, pumpkin seeds, almonds, cashews, and salt. Toss to combine.

4. Add the wet mixture to the oat mixture. Using a large spoon, toss until the oat mixture is evenly coated.

5. Pour the oats mixture onto a half sheet pan and spread into a single layer.

6. Bake for 30-40 minutes, tossing every 10 minutes, until the oats are golden brown.

7. Remove from the oven, add the mango pieces, blueberries, and cherries. Toss until all the dried fruit and oats are well combined. Allow to cool on the sheet pan, tossing every 15 minutes until completely cooled.

8. Store in an air-tight container for up to 10 days

HERE'S AN IDEA!

You can create many variations of my *Homemade Granola* to suit a specific taste or dish. If you stick to the same proportions as above (to make 6 cups), you can experiment with different combinations of ingredients. Always use rolled oats (not quick-cooking oats) as they have better flavor and texture. You can change out the honey for agave, or the canola oil for coconut oil, or the cashews for pecans—the list can go on and on. Just experiment with interesting textures and flavors! I like to add salt to my granola when I am using ingredients that are not already salted (such as plain cashews). Adjust the level of salt to suit your taste.

There are a large variety of ingredients available in the bulk section of your grocery store. Shopping in the bulk section allows you to buy the exact (or close to it) measurement of each ingredient you may want to try—thus allowing you to experiment with different combinations each time you want to make another batch of granola!

INGREDIENTS & PREP

Honey - ¼ cup

Canola Oil - ⅓ cup

Old-Fashioned Rolled Oats - 2 cups

Raw Pumpkin Seeds - ½ cup

Toasted Coconut Almonds - ½ cup

Raw Cashews - ½ cup

Sea Salt - ½ teaspoon

Dried Blueberries - ½ cup

Dried Tart Cherries - ½ cup

Dried Mango Slices - ½ cup, roughly chopped

PLANNING

Bake - 30-40 minutes, at 325 degrees F

Yield - makes 6 cups

NOTES

GOOD MORNING

Lavender Earl Grey Tea
A TIME-HONORED TRADITION ALWAYS BEST SHARED

DIRECTIONS

1. Combine the loose leaf tea and dried lavender into 2 tea infusers of your preference, and place each into a mug.
2. Pour the boiling water into the mug and allow to steep for approximately 3 minutes.
3. Remove the tea infuser, and add the desired amount of honey and cream to taste.
4. Get cozy and sip away!

Tip: If you do not have a tea infuser, a simple square of cheese cloth tied with kitchen string into a sachet will work perfectly well.

INGREDIENTS & PREP

Earl Grey Tea - 1½ tablespoons, loose leaf (your favorite variety recommended)

Dried Lavender - 2 teaspoons

Water - 24 ounces, boiling

Honey - to taste

Heavy Cream - to taste

PLANNING

Yield - serves 2

A LITTLE STORY
When I was a little boy, my nan would make me tea and toast almost every morning. I was always fascinated by the natural artwork the milk or cream made when poured into the black tea. When I was photographing this particular recipe I wanted to recreate that "artwork" to share that mesmerizingly intricate, yet simple delight, I enjoy every time I make a cup of tea.

NOTES

GOOD MORNING

Stuffed Croissants *with* Spinach
A FABULOUS SAVORY BREAKFAST, OR AS A LUNCH WITH A SALAD!

DIRECTIONS

1. Pre-heat the oven to 350 degrees F.

2. Line a half sheet pan with parchment paper. Slice each croissant horizontally along the outside curve, but not cutting all the way through—you want to make a "pocket" for the filling to nestle into. Set aside.

3. In a 10-inch sauté pan set over medium-low heat, add the olive oil and butter. Once hot, add the shallots. Cook for 2 minutes just until translucent. Add the garlic and continue to cook for another 30 seconds, being careful not to burn the garlic.

4. Next, add the chopped spinach, salt, and pepper. Cook for 3-5 minutes, stirring occasionally until the spinach is wilted and tender.

5. With a spatula, transfer the hot spinach to a small bowl and add the parmesan, mascarpone, and 2 tablespoons of Gruyère. Stir until the mascarpone is melted.

6. Next, spoon the mixture evenly into the "pocket" created in each croissant.

7. Brush the outside of each croissant with egg wash, place a spinach leaf on top of each croissant and brush again with the egg wash. Then, evenly sprinkle each croissant with the remaining 2 tablespoons of Gruyère.

8. Place onto the prepared sheet pan and bake for 7-9 minutes, until the cheese is melted and the spinach leaf is crisp. Remove from the oven and serve immediately.

IDEA
This recipe can also be served as a hot spinach dip! Instead of stuffing the spinach mixture into a croissant, put it in a heat-proof serving bowl alongside a selection of pita chips, tortilla chips, black pepper crackers, or even crisp carrot sticks.

INGREDIENTS & PREP

Plain Croissants - 2, store-bought

Olive Oil - 1 tablespoon

Butter - 1 tablespoon, unsalted

Shallot - 1 small, finely minced

Garlic - 1 clove, finely minced

Baby Spinach - 1 bag (5 ounces), fresh, roughly chopped, reserve 2 whole leaves for garnish

Sea Salt - ¼ teaspoon

Black Pepper - ¼ teaspoon, freshly cracked

Gruyère Cheese - 4 tablespoons, freshly grated, divided

Mascarpone - 2 tablespoons

Parmesan Cheese - 2 tablespoons, freshly grated (Parmigiano-Reggiano recommended)

Egg Wash - 1 extra-large egg lightly beaten with 1 tablespoon of water

PLANNING

Bake - 7-9 minutes, at 350 degrees F

Yield - serves 2

NOTES

HORS D'OEUVRE & COCKTAILS

Hors d'Oeuvre & Cocktails
COCKTAILS AND NIBBLES PERFECTED FOR TWO

Amaretto Sour Martini, 85

Baguette Pizza Bites, 87

Baked Camembert with Pears & Maple, 89

Basil French 75, 91

Beet & Parsley Canapés, 93

Classic Champagne Elixirs, 95

Dried Mango with Whipped Avocado, 97

Fig & Goat Cheese Truffles, 99

Fried Blue Cheese Olives, 101

Herbes de Provence Popcorn, 103

Homemade Ricotta, 105

Pea & Lemon Tartine, 107

Rosé Sangria with Peaches & Rosemary, 109

Salt & Pepper Potato Chips with Blue Cheese, 111

Spiced Chickpeas, 113

Spicy Garlic Edamame, 115

St-Germain Margarita, 117

Sun Dried Tomato & White Bean Spread, 119

Sweet Potato & Triple Cream Brie Tartine, 121

Yogurt, Fresh Herb & Cucumber Dip, 123

HORS D'OEUVRE & COCKTAILS

Amaretto Sour Martini

INSPIRED BY A DELICIOUS MEMORY OF THE FAIRMONT COPLEY PLAZA HOTEL IN BOSTON

DIRECTIONS

1. In a cocktail shaker, combine the amaretto, lime juice, lemon juice, honey, and a handful of ice. Shake until very cold, about 60 seconds (it is longer than you realize, but worth the work-out).

2. Pour evenly into each martini glass.

3. Serve immediately.

TIP: If you have a little extra time, fill the martini glasses with ice and place in the freezer for 10-20 minutes, or until well-chilled and frosty. This simple step makes for both an elegant presentation but also a wonderfully chilled martini!

INGREDIENTS & PREP

Amaretto – 6 ounces (Disaronno® recommended)

Lime Juice – 2 ounces, freshly squeezed

Lemon Juice – 2 ounces, freshly squeezed

Honey – 1 tablespoon

Maraschino Cherries – for garnish

PLANNING

Yield – serves 2

A LITTLE BACKSTORY

I grew up on the east coast in Massachusetts, and when I was eighteen I moved into Boston and started working for Saks Fifth Avenue. After a short time there, I became close with a small group of colleagues (many of whom are still close friends), and we would go out together after work on Friday and Saturday nights. I was the youngster of the group (meaning I was under 21—small detail!), and we would all go to hotel bars for drinks. The only cocktails I knew of then were Screwdrivers and Amaretto Sours—drinks my dad would typically order at restaurants. At the Fairmont Copley Plaza Hotel, when someone ordered an Amaretto Sour, the waiter would carry over a silver tray filled with a complete bar service for the drink, including a mini glass carafe filled with ingredients, a mini shaker, a beautiful cut-crystal martini glass, and a small bowl of cherries with silver tongs. The pomp and circumstance was just enough to make me a huge fan of this old fashioned drink. Today, just a few moons later, I am still an avid fan of this sweet, sour, and elegant martini!

NOTES

HORS D'OEUVRE & COCKTAILS

Baguette Pizza Bites

A RUSTIC AND ELEGANT HORS D'OEUVRE THAT BRINGS OUT THE KID IN US ALL!

DIRECTIONS

1. Pre-heat the oven to 400 degrees F.

2. In a small 8-inch cast iron skillet (or oven proof sauté pan), add a single layer of bread.

3. Then, over the bread, evenly distribute half of the olive oil and vodka sauce, as well as half each of the oregano, salt, pepper, red pepper flakes, both cheeses, and parsley.

4. Next, add a second layer of bread, and repeat the same steps with the remaining half of each ingredient, except the parsley (this is reserved for after it bakes).

5. Place into the oven for 8-10 minutes, or until the cheese is melted.

6. Remove from the oven, and garnish with the remaining 2 tablespoons of parsley. Serve immediately.

Tip: I always have a jar of really delicious store-bought vodka sauce and marinara sauce in the pantry for a quick and easy last-minute dinner, or for when I need a small amount for a recipe, such as this. Using a vodka sauce really adds an elegant twist to this recipe and pairs well with Fontina!

IDEA

This hors d'oeuvre is a fairly substantial dish—if you couldn't already tell! I tend to serve this when I am doing a soirée with other lighter menu items. And, *Baguette Pizza Bites* with a big green salad makes a fabulous lunch or dinner, too!

A LITTLE STORY

One of my favorite aspects of eating pasta is sopping up the sauce with big hunks of bread—a little bit of heaven never to waste! I was thinking of an hors d'oeuvre to serve to a friend that has a very refined culinary palate, and instead of doing something over-the-top fancy (as well as time consuming), I thought instead that a skillet full of crusty bread, melty cheese, vodka sauce, and just the right blend of fresh herbs could have even more of an impact! This dish is as easy as it gets, elegant, and very comforting. It is a wonderful way to bring two people together to catch up or gossip ("She did what?!") as it really is meant to share right from the skillet, with two forks and a glass of wine!

INGREDIENTS & PREP

Demi Baguette - torn into bite-sized pieces

Olive Oil - 4 tablespoons

Vodka Sauce - ¾ cup, store-bought (or your favorite red sauce)

Oregano - 2 teaspoons, dried, lightly crushed

Sea Salt - ½ teaspoon

Black Pepper - ½ teaspoon, freshly cracked

Red Pepper Flakes - ½ teaspoon (or more to add more heat)

Fontina Cheese - ¾ cup, freshly grated

Parmesan Cheese - 4 tablespoons, freshly grated (Parmigiano-Reggiano recommended)

Parsley - 4 tablespoons, fresh, roughly chopped (Italian flat leaf parsley recommended)

PLANNING

Bake - 8-10 minutes, at 400 degrees F

Yield - serves 2

NOTES

_____
_____
_____
_____
_____
_____
_____
_____

HORS D'OEUVRE & COCKTAILS

Baked Camembert *with* Pears & Maple
A TRUE GUILTY PLEASURE WRAPPED IN FLAKY BUTTERY PASTRY!

DIRECTIONS

1. Pre-heat the oven to 400 degrees F.

2. In a small sauce pan set over low heat, add the pears, maple syrup, salt, pepper, and butter. Heat until the butter is just melted. Remove from the heat and set aside.

3. On a lightly floured surface, and using a lightly floured rolling pin, roll out the sheet of puff pastry into a 12-inch square.

4. Place the wheel of Camembert in the center of the puff pastry. Beginning with a corner of the puff pastry, fold over toward the center of the wheel of Camembert. Continuing clockwise, fold the edges of the pastry up and over the cheese, working at a slight angle, overlapping each fold until the wheel of cheese is entirely enveloped.

5. Brush the entire top and sides of the pastry with egg wash and place into an 8-inch cast iron skillet. Bake for 25-30 minutes, until puffed and golden brown.

6. Remove the skillet from the oven and allow to sit for 5 minutes. Then, slowly drizzle the syrup and pear mixture around the sides of the pastry. It will sizzle a bit from the heat of the skillet.

7. Serve immediately.

INGREDIENTS & PREP

D'Anjou Pear - 1 very ripe, ¾-inch diced

Maple Syrup - ⅓ cup (Grade A recommended)

Sea Salt - ¼ teaspoon

White Pepper - ¼ teaspoon

Butter - 1 tablespoon, unsalted

Frozen Puff Pastry - 1 sheet, thawed in the refrigerator overnight

Camembert Cheese - 1 wheel (8 ounces), with rind, chilled

Egg Wash - 1 extra-large egg lightly beaten with 1 tablespoon of water

PLANNING

Bake - 25-30 minutes, at 400 degrees F

Yield - serves 2

NOTES

IDEA
You can serve this with a basket of black pepper crackers with cocktails! Cut into the pasty with a knife and have a spoon ready to serve up the gooey cheese, pastry, pears and sauce. You can even serve as a main course with a simple salad and my *French Bistro Vinaigrette* (page 133) and a crusty baguette. This could also be a tremendous cheese course for a more formal dinner party. Needless to say, I just adore this recipe not only for its incredible flavors and sumptuous texture, but also the versatility it brings to entertaining!

HORS D'OEUVRE & COCKTAILS

Basil French 75

FRESH BASIL GIVES THIS COCKTAIL A FRESH AND ELEGANT TWIST!

DIRECTIONS

1. In a cocktail shaker, combine the basil, superfine sugar, and lemon juice. Using the back of a wooden spoon, gently crush the basil for 30 seconds, which will help intensify their flavor.

2. Next, to the same shaker, add the gin, and a handful of ice. Shake until very cold, about 60 seconds (this is longer than you may realize, but worth the chill).

3. Pour evenly into glasses, and top off with Champagne.

4. Serve immediately

Tip: This is a fabulous way to use up left-over or slightly wilted basil.

IDEA

A dry Champagne (also known as brut Champagne) is really my favorite type of Champagne, simply to drink on its own, but also as an ingredient in cocktails. Champagnes all have very distinctive tastes, so take advantage of tastings at your local wine and spirits shops! This is a great way to familiarize yourself with different types of Champagne, but also wines, spirits, and other liqueurs. If you cannot find a store that offers tastings, you can also buy Champagne splits, which are smaller bottles of Champagne usually produced by some of the more popular brands, and try them that way!

IDEA

While I love making cocktails at home, I really lack the patience for complicated cocktail recipes that have more than five ingredients, or extremely specialized tools or spirits. I first had a Basil French 75 at a hotel bar in Seattle and I instantly fell in love with them! Traditionally, a French 75 is made with gin, dry Champagne, lemon juice, and simple syrup. Since I hardly ever have simple syrup in the refrigerator, but I do have a well-equipped baking station, I tried substituting super fine sugar in place of simple syrup and it works perfectly well. In fact, I use super fine sugar quite often in cocktails as it dissolves quickly and does not leave any granules behind. For an added twist on this iconic cocktail, I added fresh basil to give it a savory/sweet zing—it is perfectly bright and balanced!

INGREDIENTS & PREP

Basil - 8 leaves, fresh
Superfine Sugar - 2½ teaspoons
Lemon Juice - 1 ounce
Gin - 4 ounces
Champagne - 4 ounces, dry, well chilled

PLANNING

Yield - serves 2

NOTES

_____
_____
_____
_____
_____
_____
_____

HORS D'OEUVRE & COCKTAILS

Beet & Parsley Canapés

BRIGHTLY COLORED EARTHY BEETS CREATE A WONDERFULLY COMPLEX HORS D'OEUVRE

DIRECTIONS

1. Add all of the ingredients into the bowl of a small food processor fitted with a steel blade. Pulse until mostly smooth.

2. Serve either in a bowl or spooned onto crackers. Garnish with a sprinkle of fresh parsley.

INGREDIENTS & PREP

Beets - 8 ounces, pre-cooked, peeled, cut into quarters

Plain Greek Yogurt - 3 tablespoons

Parmesan Cheese - 2 tablespoons (Parmigiano-Reggiano recommended)

Olive Oil - 2 tablespoons

Scallions - 1 tablespoon, thinly sliced

Sliced Almonds - 1½ tablespoons

Parsley - 1 tablespoon, fresh, finely minced, plus more for garnish (Italian flat leaf parsley recommended)

Sea Salt - ¼ teaspoon

Black Pepper - ¼ teaspoon

PLANNING

Yield - makes 1½ cups

TIP

For such a small number of beets, rather than going through the hassle of cooking and peeling them, I found that buying pre-cooked beets that have been steamed and peeled (either in the freezer or refrigeration section at my grocery store) was much easier, and I really could not tell the difference between freshly cooked or store-prepared beets for this dish. You can also find them canned or in jars—just make sure they are not packed in a vinaigrette.

IDEA

Because beets have such an earthy flavor (which I just love), the addition of almonds helps to add a little texture and also a subtle nutty flavor that gives this dish more depth and roundness. My *Beet & Parsley Canapés* are wonderful to serve with other heartier things like stone wheat crackers or seeded crackers.

A LITTLE STORY

This particular canapé is so earthy and elegant, and with such unusual flavor pairings, that it all works together so incredibly deliciously! To make this hors d'oeuvre look appealing to the eye, it really does look best dolloped onto crackers and set on a white platter with a big sprinkling of fresh parsley. I love serving an elegantly presented canapé that has such an earthy flavor—it somehow has that balance of high and low that I love about cooking and entertaining!

NOTES

HORS D'OEUVRE & COCKTAILS

Classic Champagne Elixirs

CHEERS! TO A LIFE FILLED WITH GOOD FOOD, GREAT FRIENDS, AND DELICIOUS BUBBLY!

DIRECTIONS

① Fill a Champagne flute with at least 5 ounces of chilled Champagne.

② Next, choose your preferred elixir and add at least 1 ounce per Champagne flute.

③ *When using Luxardo Maraschino include a single sugar cube.

④ Garnish each flute with a raspberry.

INGREDIENTS & PREP

Champagne – 1 bottle, 750ml, very dry, chilled (your favorite)

Raspberries – 1 pint, for garnish

Sugar Cubes*

ELIXIRS
(per 5 ounces of Champagne)

Amaretto – 1 ounce

St-Germain® – 1 ounce

Raspberry Liqueur – 1 ounce (Chambord® recommended)

Orange Liqueur – 1 ounce (Grand Marnier® recommended)

Maraschino Cherry Liqueur – 1 ounce (Luxardo® Maraschino recommended)

PLANNING

Yield – serves 2

TIP
I love setting up my *Classic Champagne Elixir* bar, just for two, with different styles of Champagne flutes. This way, each time you try a new elixir you get to toast with a new and different flute.

ANOTHER TIP
You can still enjoy your favorite Champagne elixir by the glass, while preserving the remaining bottle of Champagne by using a Champagne stopper to seal in the bubbles! You can find them where Champagne and wine is sold.

TRY THIS
Creating a Champagne bar at home is a fabulous way to explore different elixirs and flavor combinations. At many wine and spirits stores you can find smaller bottles of very popular liqueurs and Champagnes, which is a wonderful way to try something new without having to invest in larger bottles. My particular favorites are listed here, although there are many other options out there! Have fun, toast, and sip the night (or afternoon!) away!

NOTES
_____
_____
_____
_____
_____
_____
_____
_____
_____

HORS D'OEUVRE & COCKTAILS

Dried Mango *with* Whipped Avocado
AMERICAN-ASIAN-FUSION CREATES THE MOST DELECTABLE CANAPÉ!

DIRECTIONS

1. In the bowl of a small food processor fitted with a steel blade, add the avocado, salt, pepper, and lime juice. Pulse until very smooth.
2. Layer each mango slice with the whipped avocado mixture and a sprinkling of wasabi peas, coconut flakes, and sesame seeds.
3. Arrange on a serving platter and serve immediately.

INGREDIENTS & PREP

Avocado – 1 (Haas variety recommended)

Lime Juice – ½ of a small lime, freshly squeezed

Sea Salt – ¼ teaspoon

Black Pepper – ¼ teaspoon

Dried Mango – 6 to 8 slices

Wasabi Peas – 2 teaspoons, finely crushed

Dried Coconut Chips – 1 tablespoon, crushed

Black Sesame Seeds – ½ teaspoon

PLANNING

Yield – serves 2

IDEA

I love serving my *Dried Mango with Whipped Avocado* accompanied with a small dish of wasabi peas to further enhance the spicy heat! They both pair perfectly with a dry white wine, a light Japanese beer such as Sapporo, or even a warm Japanese sake in the winter.

A LITTLE STORY

During the time I was testing recipes for this cookbook, I visited our closest friends in Hawaii a few times, and each time I brought back with me to Chicago amazing inspiration with Asian-infused flavors. Our friends live just near Chinatown in Honolulu, where the streets are bustling with fresh food markets filled with fruits and vegetables, interesting restaurants (my favorite Vietnamese Pho place, Pho'Hana!), and countless stalls filled with cooking equipment and little omiyage—little keepsakes to bring back to give to friends from your trip. Originally, I made this recipe with fresh mango and in a "tartar" presentation, which was very good. However, I discovered that finding fresh mangos wasn't always easy (particularly in the winter in the Midwest). Dried mangos are now readily available in most grocery stores where dried fruits and nuts are found, and make both a fantastic presentation and consistent flavor and texture.

NOTES

HORS D'OEUVRE & COCKTAILS

Fig & Goat Cheese Truffles
THIS SAVORY TWIST ON THE CLASSIC SWEET TRUFFLE WILL BE A SURPRISE HIT!

DIRECTIONS

1. In a small bowl, add the goat cheese, preserves, salt, and pepper. Mix until well combined. Cover and chill in the refrigerator for 1 hour.

2. Meanwhile, in a 10-inch sauté pan set over medium heat, add the whole pistachios. Toast for 4-6 minutes, or until lightly browned. You will know when they are done when you begin to smell their wonderful aroma. Once the pistachios are toasted, remove them from the pan and give them a rough chop. Set aside in a shallow dish.

3. Next, using a 1-inch scoop or tablespoon, scoop out balls of the chilled goat cheese mixture and place onto a half sheet pan lined with parchment paper.

4. After you have scooped all the goat cheese mixture, roll each one lightly by hand into a ball, and then roll each ball through the chopped pistachios to evenly coat.

5. Arrange the rolled coated truffles on a serving platter and serve.

INGREDIENTS & PREP

Goat Cheese – 5 ounces, at room temperature

Fig Preserves – 2 tablespoons

Fleur de Sel – ¼ teaspoon

Black Pepper – ¼ teaspoon, freshly cracked

Pistachios – ½ cup, shelled

PLANNING

Yield – makes 10 truffles

TIP
The goat cheese mixture will stay fresh for up to 5 days in the refrigerator. Simply roll truffles as you need or want to serve them. If you roll the truffles with the pistachios and then refrigerate, the nuts will become soft and lose their crunch.

IDEA
I like to serve these little bites of fig goodness in small paper candy cups. They have a soft and velvety texture, and the paper cups help to make them easier to handle.

NOTES

HORS D'OEUVRE & COCKTAILS

Fried Blue Cheese Olives
THE QUINTESSENTIAL NIBBLE, PERFECT WITH COCKTAILS

DIRECTIONS

1. In a small sauce pan set over high heat, add the oil. Line a plate with a layer of paper towels. Set aside.

2. Place the lightly beaten egg in a small, shallow bowl. In an additional small bowl, add the bread crumbs.

3. Roll each olive through the egg, then through the breadcrumbs to evenly coat. Coat all of the olives and set aside together.

4. Once the oil has reached 350 degrees F (use a candy thermometer to be accurate), and working in small batches, gently place the olives in the hot oil. Once golden brown, remove the olives with a small slotted spoon and place on the plate prepared with paper towel to drain.

5. Allow to sit for 5 minutes before serving.

INGREDIENTS & PREP

Canola Oil - 1½ cups

Egg - 1 extra-large, lightly beaten

Dried Breadcrumbs - ½ cup, plain

Blue Cheese Olives - 16, patted dry, at room temperature

PLANNING

Yield - makes 16 olives

TIP
I am *gaga* over making these at home! They are so simple and such an unexpected little nibble with cocktails. Serve my *Fried Blue Cheese Olives* piled high in a little silver or crystal nut dish. You can find small nut dishes online, at flea markets, and even at estate or yard sales. You can also insert a pick into each olive and line them in a perfect little row on a small rectangular plater.

A LITTLE STORY
One of my favorite neighborhood spots in Chicago is RL, which is where I first had fried blue cheese olives! Whenever Ryan and I (or any of my +1s) would go for a meal or sit at their cozy bar, we always ordered these little bites of crispy and briny heaven. When they were retired from the RL menu I knew I needed to work out how to make my own version at home. My *Fried Blue Cheese Olives* have just the right amount of crispiness from the breadcrumb coating, and are soft and pillowy when you bite into them! If you don't like blue cheese stuffed olives, you can certainly use another variety such as garlic, almond, or even jalapeño! You could even make an entire batch using various stuffed versions!

NOTES

HORS D'OEUVRE & COCKTAILS

Herbes *de* Provence Popcorn
SIMPLY THE EASIEST AND YET MOST SOPHISTICATED NIBBLE POSSIBLE!

DIRECTIONS

1. In a small saucepan set over low heat, add the butter and Herbes de Provence. Heat until the butter is just melted. Remove from the heat and set aside.

2. Prepare the popcorn according to package directions. Once popped and still hot, empty the bag into a large bowl.

3. Drizzle over the melted butter and herbs. Sprinkle over the salt, pepper, and parsley.

4. Toss until the popcorn is completely mixed.

5. Serve immediately.

Tip: For an even more decadent version, prepare the popcorn as above and also add 1 tablespoon of freshly grated Parmesan cheese!

INGREDIENTS & PREP

Popcorn – 1 microwavable bag, plain

Butter – 2 tablespoons

Herbes de Provence – 1 teaspoon, lightly crushed

Fleur de Sel – ¼ teaspoon

Black Pepper – ¼ teaspoon

Parsley – 1 tablespoon, fresh, finely minced (Italian flat leaf parsley recommended)

PLANNING

Yield – serves 2

IDEA
Herbes de Provence is found where dried herbs are sold in almost all grocery stores. If you can't find it in your local store, it is readily available online and in specialty food stores. It is a wonderful dried herb mix to have on hand in your panty. It has incredible flavor with a savory note and floral aroma. It is the star ingredient in my *Roasted Cauliflower Soup*, page 139.

A LITTLE STORY
Hotel bars around the world serve little silver bowls filled with nibbles like wasabi peas, roasted nuts, thick-cut salty potato chips, and even black pepper popcorn, to name just a few I have enjoyed on my travels. Herbes de Provence Popcorn was inspired by those chicest of hotel bars with fantastic cocktails and a vibe that captures to high life. The dried herb blend Herbes de Provence is such a fabulous ingredient to have on hand! This South of France signature seasoning is a blend of aromatic herbs, including lavender, basil, rosemary, thyme, oregano, tarragon, parsley, fennel seed, marjoram, and sage. It is distinctive yet delicate when used in the right proportion. When you combine it with warm butter, a little salt and pepper, and finely minced fresh parsley, it is a fabulously elegant way to give simple popcorn amazing pizzazz!

NOTES

_____
_____
_____
_____
_____
_____
_____
_____

HORS D'OEUVRE & COCKTAILS

Homemade Ricotta

CREAMY AND FULL OF SWEET FLAVOR, WITH A LIGHT AND DREAMY TEXTURE

DIRECTIONS

1. In a large sauce pan set over medium-high heat add the milk, cream, and sea salt.

2. Allow the liquid to come to a full boil, then remove it from the heat and add the lemon juice. Let it rest for 5 minutes to allow the curds and whey to separate.

3. In the meantime, line a fine mesh sieve with 6 layers of damp cheesecloth. Then set it over a very large bowl.

4. After the 5 minutes rest, pour the milk mixture into the cheesecloth and allow the cheese to drain for at least 2 hours in the refrigerator. During the draining time, fold the ends of the cheesecloth over the top of cheese and gently press to expel excess liquid. Do this at least 4 times. This will ensure you have an extremely luxurious and creamy ricotta.

5. Transfer the cheese from the cheesecloth into a serving bowl, being sure to scrape the cheese from the sides of the cheesecloth.

6. Garnish with a big drizzle of olive oil and salt and pepper, and serve.

INGREDIENTS & PREP

Whole Milk – 4 cups
Heavy Cream – 2 cups
Sea Salt – ½ teaspoon
Lemon Juice – ¼ cup, freshly squeezed

PLANNING

Yield – makes 1½ cups

TIP
While you drain the cheese, depending on the size of the bowl, you may have to empty the liquid a few times to ensure it drains completely. You can store my *Homemade Ricotta* in an air-tight container and store in the refrigerator for up to 3 days.

IDEA
I love serving my *Homemade Ricotta* alongside fig and olive crackers, or something with great texture. A little jar of honey on the plate is another delicious addition as it adds a different type of sweetness and really stands up well to the olive oil. This ricotta is so creamy and delicious that you can really layer it with so many flavors.

NOTES

HORS D'OEUVRE & COCKTAILS

Pea & Lemon Tartine

THE ESSENCE OF FRESH AND FLAVORFUL INGREDIENTS, PERFECT ON CRUSTY BREAD!

DIRECTIONS

1. Toast the bread slices in a toaster until golden brown. Set aside.
2. Fill a bowl with very hot tap water. Place all of the frozen peas into the water and allow to sit for 5 minutes. Strain the peas.
3. In the bowl of a mini food processor fitted with a steel blade, add 1¼ cups of peas, crème fraîche, salt, pepper, and ½ teaspoon of lemon zest. Process until well blended. The mixture should still have a chunky texture.
4. Next, spread the green pea mixture evenly onto one side of each toasted bread slice and evenly top with the remaining 2 tablespoons of whole green peas, grated cucumber, dill, chives, and the remaining ½ teaspoon of lemon zest.
5. Drizzle lightly with olive oil to finish. Sprinkle with more sea salt and black pepper to taste. Serve.

INGREDIENTS & PREP

French Boule - 2 large slices (you can also use Sourdough, Wheat, or Tuscan Pane)

Green Peas - 1¼ cups, plus 2 tablespoons, frozen

Crème Fraîche - 2 tablespoons

Sea Salt - ¼ teaspoon

Black Pepper - ¼ teaspoon, freshly cracked

Lemon Zest - 1 teaspoon, divided

Persian Cucumber - 4 tablespoons, grated

Dill - 1 teaspoon, fresh, roughly chopped

Chives - 2 teaspoons, fresh, finely chopped

Olive Oil - to drizzle for finishing

PLANNING

Yield - serves 2

TIP

I love to use Persian Cucumbers both in my cooking and serving with dips. They are very small, tender, and have great flavor that works well in recipes where cucumbers are called for. They are especially useful when cooking for two as they are just the right size for my recipes with hardly anything leftover. If you cannot find Persian Cucumbers, you can also use an English Cucumber. If neither of those are available, a regular cucumber will indeed still work. Just make sure to peel and remove the seeds as they tend to be bitter in the regular variety of cucumber.

IDEA

My *Pea & Lemon Tartine* is certainly hearty enough to be served as a light lunch with a green salad. For cocktail hour, slice it on the diagonal for a more elegant presentation. Arrange the slices on a serving platter or on a cutting board. The flavors of the tartine pair very well with an oaky Chardonnay, a dry Rosé, or a light Pinot Noir.

NOTES

HORS D'OEUVRE & COCKTAILS

Rosé Sangria *with* Peaches & Rosemary
REFRESHINGLY LIGHT WITH A SWEET AND SAVORY TWIST

DIRECTIONS

1. Pour the Rosé and Triple Sec into a large glass pitcher.
2. Add the honey and sugar. Stir until completely dissolved.
3. Next, add the peaches and rosemary.
4. Chill in the refrigerator for at least 3 hours.
5. Just before serving, add the chilled Champagne to the pitcher.
6. Serve immediately.

Tip: To garnish each glass, add fresh rosemary springs and the "boozy" peach wedges.

INGREDIENTS & PREP

Rosé - 375ml (half bottle)

Triple Sec - ¼ cup

Honey - 2 teaspoons

Superfine Sugar - 2 teaspoons

Peaches - 2, pitted, each cut into 8 wedges

Rosemary - 3 sprigs, fresh, each approximately 4-inches, plus more for garnish

Champagne - 375ml (half bottle), chilled

PLANNING

Yield - serves 2

FOOD FOR THOUGHT
Sangria is typically a chilled drink served in Spain and Portugal during the summer months - consisting of wine, fruit, brandy or liqueur, and a sweetener. Using a combination of honey and sugar helps this recipe have more flavor from the subtle rich sweetness of honey without being overly sugary.

NOTES

HORS D'OEUVRE & COCKTAILS

Salt & Pepper Potato Chips *with* Blue Cheese
SOMETIMES SIMPLE IS THE BEST, WITH AN UNEXPECTED "WOW!" FACTOR

DIRECTIONS

1. Pre-heat the oven to 400 degrees F.
2. In an 8-inch cast iron skillet, or other oven-proof serving dish, add half of the potato chips. Then evenly scatter over the chips 1 ounce of blue cheese, 1 tablespoon of chives, and ¾ teaspoon of lemon zest.
3. Add another layer of potato chips and the remaining blue cheese.
4. Place in the oven for 4-6 minutes, or until the cheese is melted.
5. Remove from the oven, and sprinkle with the remaining chives and lemon zest. Serve hot.

INGREDIENTS & PREP

Salt & Pepper Potato Chips - 4 ounces, store-bought

Blue Cheese - 2 ounces, crumbled (Stilton recommended)

Chives - 2 tablespoons, fresh, finely chopped

Lemon Zest - 1½ teaspoons, freshly zested

PLANNING

Bake - 4-6 minutes, at 400 degrees F

Yield - serves 2

TIP
Any brand of Salt & Pepper potato chips will work for this recipe. Using a small cast iron skillet allows this dish to go from oven to table, just remember to use a trivet to protect your tabletop!

IDEA
I love the addition of Stilton for this dish - it is a perfect paring with a glass of very dry Champagne or bold red wine, to sip and enjoy with your +1.

NOTES

HORS D'OEUVRE & COCKTAILS

Spiced Chickpeas
A FUN SAVORY ADDITION TO COCKTAIL HOUR!

DIRECTIONS

1. Pre-heat the oven to 450 degrees F.

2. In a medium bowl, add the chickpeas, cayenne pepper, smoked paprika, sea salt, and garlic powder. Stir to coat evenly.

3. Place the chickpeas onto a half sheet pan, in a single layer. Drizzle over the olive oil. Shake the pan to thoroughly coat the chickpeas with the olive oil.

4. Bake for 12-15 minutes, or until the chickpeas are golden and crisp.

5. Remove the sheet pan from the oven, sprinkle over more salt and garlic powder to taste, toss to coat evenly, and transfer to a serving bowl. Serve warm.

INGREDIENTS & PREP

Chickpeas – 1 can (15 ounces), drained, rinsed, patted dry with a paper towel

Cayenne Pepper – ½ teaspoon

Smoked Paprika – ¾ teaspoon

Sea Salt – ½ teaspoon, plus more to garnish

Garlic Powder – ½ teaspoon, plus more to garnish

Olive Oil – 1 tablespoon

PLANNING

Bake – 12-15 minutes, at 450 degrees F

Yield – serves 2

TIP
My *Spiced Chickpeas* really are best when roasted just before you want to serve them – they are slightly crisp on the outside and have a very pillowy texture inside. After they have cooled for a while, they tend to toughen.

IDEA
I like to serve my *Spiced Chickpeas* with cocktails, use them to spice up salads (literally!) in rice dishes, and even as a side dish. They are so versatile and add great flavor and texture to any menu!

A SHORT STORY
I first had these at a friend's dinner party and after just a few bites I knew I had to try to make them myself at home! I found that adding smoked paprika and garlic powder really helps to give a depth of flavor, more than just being spicy. These certainly do have a kick, but there is just the right amount of heat to balance the great flavor.

NOTES

HORS D'OEUVRE & COCKTAILS

Spicy Garlic Edamame

FORGET THOSE NUTS, THESE ARE YOUR NEW FAVORITE NIBBLE FOR COCKTAIL HOUR!

DIRECTIONS

1. Pre-heat the oven to 450 degrees F.

2. Place the defrosted edamame onto a half sheet pan. Toss with the olive oil and salt. Spread into a single layer and roast for 15-20 minutes, tossing once half way through the baking time.

3. Remove the edamame from the oven and transfer to a large bowl. Add the red pepper flakes and minced garlic. Toss to evenly coat. Garnish with more salt to taste.

4. Serve hot or warm.

INGREDIENTS & PREP

Edamame - 1 bag (14 ounces), in pods, defrosted

Olive Oil - 1 tablespoon

Sea Salt - 1½ teaspoons

Red Pepper Flakes - 2 teaspoons

Garlic - 3 tablespoons, jarred minced

PLANNING

Bake - 15-20 minutes, at 450 degrees F

Yield - serves 2

TIP
I usually do not use jarred minced garlic when cooking, as I very much prefer fresh garlic, but I found that for this recipe the jarred version was perfect. It may have something to do with it being both finely minced and the very wet consistency. The garlic coats each pod of edamame better than minced fresh garlic and has a slightly less raw flavor than fresh garlic, helping to make this the perfect finger-food.

IDEA
If you are not a fan of spicy food, you can certainly adjust the degree of heat by adding a smaller amount of red pepper flakes. I prefer the hot end of the spectrum and sometimes add even more for a seriously intense hit! You can really turn up the flavor volume with the addition of a little freshly grated lime zest—if you are heavy-handed like me with the red pepper flakes, the lime zest is a great way to cut the spice and balance out the dish.

NOTES

HORS D'OEUVRE & COCKTAILS

St-Germain Margarita
A SOPHISTICATED VARIATION OF A CLASSIC COCKTAIL

DIRECTIONS

① After you have squeezed the lime for its juice, rub the cut lime around the rims of 2 double old fashioned glasses (or glasses of your choice).

② Pour a small amount of Fleur de Sel onto a small plate, and spread evenly. Carefully dip the rim of each glass into the salt. Fill each glass with ice. Set aside.

③ In a cocktail shaker, combine the tequila, St-Germain liqueur, lime juice, and a handful of ice. Shake until very cold, about 60 seconds.

④ Pour evenly into each glass, and serve immediately.

Tip: If you cannot find Fleur de Sel, you can use a course sea salt.

INGREDIENTS & PREP
Lime - 1 ounce juice, freshly squeezed
Silver Tequila - 2 ounces
Fleur de Sel - for salted rim
St-Germain® - 5 ounces

PLANNING
Yield - serves 2

IDEA
This recipe can easily be doubled, or tripled. Just make as many batches as you would like and pour them into a glass pitcher. Then, when you are ready to serve, shake each cocktail over ice for that final chill.

A LITTLE NOTE
St-Germain® is a French brand of liqueur flavored with elderflowers, which are small flowers that bloom on the hillsides of the French Alps during a particularly brief six-week period each spring. The liqueur is very aromatic and lightly sweet, and pairs perfectly with freshly squeezed citrus, which livens up this margarita! While this is not an "elderflower margarita," it is instead a margarita with a hint of elderflower. My St-Germain Margarita is a very elegant cocktail, perfect for sipping. The addition of the Fleur de Sel salted rim, which gives a briny taste – like the ocean, instead of a harsher "salty" taste – makes this an over-the-top luxurious cocktail perfect for entertaining!

NOTES

HORS D'OEUVRE & COCKTAILS

Sun Dried Tomato & White Bean Spread

A ROBUST AND FLAVORFUL SPREAD MADE WITH EVERYDAY GROCERY STORE INGREDIENTS

DIRECTIONS

1. Place all of the ingredients into the bowl of a small food processor. Pulse until well blended, but still chunky.
2. Transfer to a small bowl and serve.

INGREDIENTS & PREP

Cannellini Beans - 1 can (15 ounces), drained, rinsed

Sun Dried Tomatoes - 1 tablespoon, roughly chopped (preferably packed in oil)

Garlic - 1 clove, finely minced

Basil - 1 tablespoon, roughly chopped

Red Pepper Flakes - ⅛ teaspoon

Sea Salt - ¼ teaspoon

Black Pepper - ¼ teaspoon, freshly cracked

Olive Oil - 3 tablespoons, from the jar of sun dried tomatoes

Balsamic Vinegar - 1 teaspoon

Parmesan Cheese - 1 tablespoon (Parmigiano-Reggiano recommended)

PLANNING

Yield - makes 1½ cups

TIP
My *Sun Dried Tomato & White Bean Spread* will stay fresh refrigerated in an air-tight container for up to 3 days.

IDEA
In addition to serving this spread as a hors d'oeuvre with crackers, it is also fabulous as a bruschetta on toasted baguette slices with diced tomatoes and a drizzle of olive oil, or as a spread on sandwiches.

Serving homemade hors d'oeuvre and appetizers does not have to be complicated. In fact, when I am entertaining larger crowds I usually serve a combination of store-bought nibbles and one very simple (but flavorful) homemade dish. My *Sun Dried Tomato & White Bean Spread* simply could not be any easier to prepare and is bursting with flavorful ingredients—do not let the simple white bean fool you! I even use the olive oil from the jar of sun dried tomatoes to bump up the flavor!

NOTES

HORS D'OEUVRE & COCKTAILS

Sweet Potato & Triple Cream Tartine

A RUSTIC AND EARTHY COMBINATION OF INGREDIENTS FOR A COMFORTINGLY ELEGANT DISH

DIRECTIONS

1. Toast the bread slices in a toaster until golden brown. Place them onto a half sheet pan lined with a sheet of parchment paper. Set aside.

2. In a 10-inch sauté pan set over medium heat, add 3 tablespoons of olive oil. Once hot, add the sweet potatoes, salt, and pepper. Cover and cook for 8-10 minutes, tossing occasionally, or until tender and the edges are lightly browned.

3. Next, add the additional tablespoon of olive oil to the pan and add the shallots. Cook, uncovered, for another 2 minutes. Then add the garlic and continue to cook for another 30 seconds.

4. Transfer to a small bowl. Set aside.

5. Set the broiler to high.

6. Top one side of each toasted bread slice evenly with sweet potatoes. Then, dot the top of each one with Brie and place under the broiler for 30-60 seconds, or until the Brie is melted.

7. Remove from the broiler, and sprinkle with basil, and more salt and pepper to taste. Serve.

TIP
If you are not a fan of Brie, you can substitute with cubes of Gruyère, White Cheddar, or Fontina. You may have to adjust the broiling temperature and timing – keep your eye on them when they are under the broiler, you are looking for the cheese to melt and brown just lightly.

INGREDIENTS & PREP

French Boule – 2 large slices (you can also use Sourdough, Wheat, or Tuscan Pane)

Olive Oil – 4 tablespoons, divided

Sweet Potato – 1 large, peeled, ½-inch diced

Sea Salt – ¼ teaspoon

Black Pepper – ¼ teaspoon, freshly cracked

Shallot – 1 medium, roughly chopped

Garlic – 2 cloves, finely minced

Triple Cream Brie Cheese – 3 ounces, chilled, cut into ½-inch pieces

Basil – ¼ cup, fresh, roughly chopped

PLANNING

Broiler – set to high

Yield – serves 2

NOTES

HORS D'OEUVRE & COCKTAILS

Yogurt, Fresh Herb & Cucumber Dip
A BRIGHTLY FLAVORED DIP FILLED WITH FRESH INGREDIENTS

DIRECTIONS

1. Place all of the prepared ingredients into a small bowl. Whisk until everything is well mixed.

2. Serve with pita chips, as part of a crudité platter, or with Indian Naan bread.

TIP
In most grocery stores, either in the freezer section or bread aisle, you can find pre-made Indian Naan bread. It is a delicious flatbread with a pillowy inside and crispy bottom. You can find them plain, or flavored with garlic, onions, and other wonderful combinations. Naan is a great alternative to the usual dipping options, and depending on the version you choose, can complement my *Yogurt, Fresh Herb & Cucumber Dip* with great flavors of its own.

A LITTLE SOMETHING EXTRA
If you cannot find naan bread in your area, you can use regular pita bread. Pre-heat the oven to 375 degrees F. Brush the pita bread with olive oil, and place it on a half sheet pan. Bake it for 5-10 minutes or until crisp, turning once. Remove the sheet pan from the oven and rub the toasted pita bread with a fresh garlic clove.

INGREDIENTS & PREP

Greek Yogurt - ¾ cup, plain

Mayonnaise - ¼ cup

Persian Cucumber - ½ cup, grated

Dill - 2 teaspoons, fresh, finely minced

Parsley - 1 teaspoon, fresh, finely minced (Italian flat leaf parsley recommended)

Scallions - 3 teaspoons, finely minced

Lemon Zest - ¼ teaspoon, freshly zested

Sea Salt - ¼ teaspoon

Black Pepper - ½ teaspoon

Tabasco - 5 dashes (or more to add more heat)

Cumin - ⅛ teaspoon

PLANNING

Yield - makes 1½ cups

NOTES

SOUPS & SALADS

Soups & Salads
FRESH AND FLAVORFUL FIRST COURSES

Artichoke & Tomato Salad, 127

Asparagus Soup, 129

Butternut Squash & Black Bean Soup, 131

French Bistro Vinaigrette, 133

Lentil Stew, 135

Matchstick Apple Salad, 137

Roasted Cauliflower Soup, 139

Roasted Fruit with Rosemary Vinaigrette, 141

Warm White Bean Salad, 143

SOUPS & SALADS

Artichoke & Tomato Salad

A HEARTY SALAD THAT HIGHLIGHTS PERFECTLY RIPE TOMATOES

DIRECTIONS

1. Pre-heat the broiler to the highest setting.

2. Place the torn bread pieces onto a half sheet pan. Set it under the broiler for just 20-30 seconds, or until the edges of the bread just begin to turn golden brown. Keep your eye on the bread as it will burn very quickly.

3. Place the artichoke hearts and tomatoes down the center of a serving platter or bowl. Evenly sprinkle with parsley, basil, salt, pepper, and Parmesan shavings.

4. Scatter the bread over the salad. Drizzle 2-3 tablespoons of the artichoke brine over the entire salad. Serve.

INGREDIENTS & PREP

Baguette – 1½ cups, torn into roughly 1-inch pieces

Marinated Artichoke Hearts – 1 jar (12 ounces), reserve the brine

Heirloom Tomato – 1 large, fresh, sliced ½-inch thick

Parsley – ¼ cup, fresh, whole leaves (Italian flat leaf parsley recommended)

Basil – 1 tablespoon, fresh, roughly chopped

Sea Salt – ½ teaspoon

Black Pepper – ½ teaspoon, freshly cracked

Parmesan Cheese – ½ cup, large shavings (Parmigiano-Reggiano recommended)

PLANNING

Broiler – set to high

Yield – serves 2

TIP
I sometimes also enjoy adding freshly grated lemon zest to this salad. Just mix ¾ teaspoon of zest into the few tablespoons of brine before you drizzle it over the salad. If you want to add a little heat, add ½ teaspoon of crushed red pepper flakes for a fabulous additional dimension.

IDEA
This salad is particularly good during tomato season! If you cannot find larger tomatoes with great flavor, use grape or cherry tomatoes instead and cut them in half lengthwise.

FOOD FOR THOUGHT
Whenever I think of serving anything with artichoke hearts, especially in a salad, I often use a really good jar of marinated artichokes from the grocery store. Not only do you get flavorful artichoke hearts with nearly zero effort for your salad, but you can also use the delicious herbed brine they are packed in to give the salad even more zing!

NOTES

SOUPS & SALADS

Asparagus Soup

A SMOOTH AND SOPHISTICATED SOUP, PERFECT TO BEGIN AN ELEGANT MEAL

DIRECTIONS

1. In a medium Dutch oven or heavy-bottomed pan set over medium heat, add the olive oil and 1 tablespoon of butter. Once hot, add the red onion, salt, and pepper. Cook for 5 minutes stirring occasionally, until the onions are tender.

2. Add the asparagus (reserving the tips) to the pan and cook for another 3-4 minutes, stirring occasionally.

3. Then, add the garlic and cook for just 1 minute more, being careful not to burn the garlic.

4. Next, add the stock and bring the soup to a boil. Then reduce the heat, cover, and simmer for 10-15 minutes, or until the asparagus is very soft.

5. Meanwhile, in a small sauté pan set over medium heat, add the remaining tablespoon of butter. Once hot, add the reserved asparagus tips and sauté for 3-4 minutes, until just tender. Remove from the heat. String the asparagus tips onto a wooden skewer and set aside.

6. Once the asparagus is very tender, remove the pan from the heat. Use a stick blender directly in the pan and blend until smooth. (You can also use a food processor or blender.)

7. Once all of the soup is blended, pour it through a fine mesh sieve set over a heat-proof bowl. Then, pour the strained soup back into the pot and whisk in the crème fraiche. Gently re-heat, if desired.

8. Ladle the soup into bowls, garnish each with one of the skewers, and a generous sprinkle of Parmesan cheese and serve.

TIP
I do realize that the color of my *Asparagus Soup* is like the color of a kitchen appliance from the '70s (and that is me being nice!). However, the flavor and texture is so elegant that it is worth a little effort to jazz it up and make its appearance a little more appealing to the eye. The sautéed asparagus tips on a skewer not only add a bit of fresh color, but declares what is in the soup, and acts as an edible garnish.

INGREDIENTS & PREP

Olive Oil - 1 tablespoon

Butter - 2 tablespoons, unsalted, divided

Red Onion - half of a small red onion, ½-inch diced

Sea Salt - ¾ teaspoon

Black Pepper - ½ teaspoon

Asparagus - 1 pound, trimmed, cut into 1-inch lengths, tips reserved

Garlic - 2 cloves, finely minced

Vegetable Stock - 2½ cups

Crème Fraîche - ¼ cup

Parmesan Cheese - for garnish, freshly grated (Parmigiano-Reggiano recommended)

PLANNING

Yield - serves 2

NOTES

SOUPS & SALADS

Butternut Squash & Black Bean Soup
COLORFUL, HEARTY, AND HEALTHY!

DIRECTIONS

① In a medium Dutch oven or heavy-bottomed pan set over medium heat, add the olive oil. Once hot, add the onions, red peppers, thyme, rosemary, salt, black pepper, and red pepper flakes. Cook for 8-10 minutes stirring occasionally, or until the onions are just tender.

② Next, add the butternut squash and cook for another 3-4 minutes, stirring occasionally.

③ Then add the garlic and continue cooking for another 1-2 minutes, being careful not to burn the garlic.

④ Add the stock to the pan and bring to a boil. Then reduce the heat and simmer, and cook for 7-10 minutes, or until the squash is just tender.

⑤ Lastly, off the heat, stir in the black beans, spinach, and smoked paprika. The residual heat from the soup will warm through the beans and wilt the spinach.

⑥ Ladle each portion into bowls, garnish with generous sprinkle of Parmesan cheese, and serve.

TIP
My *Butternut Squash & Black Bean Soup* is a wonderful base to build on. If black beans just don't excite you, swap them out for white beans, cannellini beans, or just leave them out. The same goes for the other vegetables. However, you may have to adjust the cooking times of other vegetables.

A THOUGHT
This soup is just loaded with flavor, color, and texture! I especially love the butternut squash as I cook them very al dente so they still have great texture and stand up well when cooking away in the soup.

INGREDIENTS & PREP

Olive Oil - 2 tablespoons

Yellow Onion - 1 small, ½-inch diced

Red Pepper - 1 small, ½-inch diced

Thyme - 1 teaspoon, fresh, finely minced

Rosemary - 1 teaspoon, fresh, finely minced

Sea Salt - ¾ teaspoon

Black Pepper - ¾ teaspoon

Red Pepper Flakes - ¼ teaspoon

Butternut Squash - 12 ounces, peeled, seeded, cut into ¾-inch cubes

Garlic - 2 cloves, finely minced

Vegetable Stock - 2 cups

Black Beans - 1 can (15 ounces), drained, well rinsed

Baby Spinach - 3 ounces, fresh

Smoked Paprika - ½ teaspoon

Parmesan Cheese - for garnish, freshly grated (Parmigiano-Reggiano recommended)

PLANNING
Yield - serves 2

NOTES
_____
_____
_____
_____
_____
_____
_____

SOUPS & SALADS

French Bistro Vinaigrette
A LITTLE BIT OF A PARIS BISTRO, AT HOME!

DIRECTIONS

1. Place all of the prepared ingredients into a jar with a tight-fitting lid. Shake vigorously for about 60 seconds. Refrigerate for at least 30 minutes before dressing a salad.

A LITTLE STORY

Every time I am in Paris, I am mesmerized at how simple and delicious the classic bistro food is! The menus are long and extensive, but each and every dish seems to be accompanied by a petite salad dressed in a light and creamy vinaigrette – the iconic French creamy mustard vinaigrette. There are thousands of cookbooks and online recipes for this classic vinaigrette, with just as many variations of ingredients and measurements. And truth be told, some of the ones I tried are really very good, just not what I remember from my Parisian restaurant adventures.

So, I set off on a vinaigrette journey, armed with an obscene amount of oils, jars of different mustards, whisks, and measuring cups. Batches and batches later, I finally developed a few small but important tricks to recreate this iconic dressing at home in Chicago (and now where you are!). There are a couple magic ingredients and key techniques: Crème fraîche, a combination of both olive oil and vegetable oil, and a garlic press. Adding crème fraîche gave the dressing more of a creaminess and tang, like what I remembered from Paris. When I left it out, there was a noticeable absence in both texture and flavor.

Also, instead on mincing the garlic, I found that using a garlic press turned the garlic into almost a paste which incorporated into the dressing much better. Finally, adding a combination of both the olive oil and vegetable oil was, I my opinion, the most crucial magic ingredient to arriving at my French Bistro Vinaigrette. Using all olive oil was too heavy in taste, and using all vegetable oil was lacking in flavor. Using both was the perfect combination!

Making my *French Bistro Vinaigrette* doesn't take more than five minutes, and it is the perfect accompaniment to a variety of salads, even with roasted vegetables and fruit, and as a "sauce" for my **Butternut Squash Medallions with Wilted Spinach**, page 173. It is also quite lovely to decorate a cheese plate – the mustard really comes through the dressing and amps up the flavors of certain cheeses, such as Gruyère. It is also fabulous to serve alongside a crudité platter.

INGREDIENTS & PREP

Egg Yolk – 1 extra-large, at room temperature

Sea Salt – ½ teaspoon

Black Pepper – ½ teaspoon, freshly cracked

Champagne Vinegar – 2 tablespoons

Crème Fraîche – 1 tablespoon

Dijon Mustard – 2 teaspoons

Garlic – 1 clove, crushed with a garlic press

Canola Oil – 7 tablespoons

Olive Oil – 1 tablespoon

PLANNING

Yield – makes 1¼ cups

NOTES

SOUPS & SALADS

Lentil Stew

A WONDERFUL MIX OF FRESH VEGETABLES AND EARTHY FRENCH LENTILS!

DIRECTIONS

1. In a medium Dutch oven or heavy-bottomed pan set over medium heat, add the olive oil. Once hot, add the potatoes, carrots, leeks, salt, and pepper. Cook for 5 minutes, until the vegetables are just tender.

2. Next, add the garlic and thyme and cook for another 1 minute, being careful not to burn the garlic.

3. Add the stock and lentils. Bring to a boil, then reduce the heat, cover, and simmer for 30-40 minutes, until the lentils are just tender, but still have a bite to them. During the last 5 minutes of cooking the lentils, stir in the green beans and corn.

4. Once the lentils are done, remove the pan from the heat and stir in the tomatoes and parsley. Serve hot.

INGREDIENTS & PREP

Olive Oil – 3 tablespoons

Purple Potatoes – 3 small, ¾-inch diced

Carrot – 1 medium, peeled, ¾-inch diced

Leeks – 1 cup (about 1 large stalk), white and light green parts, ¾-inch diced

Sea Salt – ½ teaspoon

Black Pepper – ½ teaspoon

Garlic – 2 cloves, finely minced

Thyme – 1 teaspoon, fresh, roughly chopped

Vegetable Stock – 3¼ cups

French Green Lentils – 1 cup, rinsed, drained

French Green Beans – 5-ounces, ends trimmed, cut into 1-inch lengths on the diagonal

Sweet Corn – 1 large ear, kernels only

Roma Tomatoes – 1 cup, cored, seeded, ¾-inch diced

Parsley – ¼ cup, fresh, finely minced (Italian flat leaf parsley recommended)

PLANNING

Yield – serves 2

NOTES

FOOD FOR THOUGHT

Soup for a meal, or at least as part of one, makes me almost as happy as having French fries and Champagne (I said almost!). My *Lentil Stew* is filled with colorful flavorful vegetables and perfectly al dente French lentils. French lentils in a soup or stew create a thick and almost creamy consistency. I prefer not to purée this soup and to leave it very chunky. However, you can certainly use a stick blender, food processor, or even a traditional blender and purée to your desired consistency.

SOUPS & SALADS

Matchstick Apple Salad
A CLASSIC SALAD WITH A VINAIGRETTE TWIST!

DIRECTIONS

1. Start by placing the cut apples in a large bowl of cold water. Add the lemon juice, and allow to sit until ready to serve.

2. Meanwhile, mix the vinegar, honey, cinnamon, salt, and pepper in a small bowl. Slowly drizzle in the olive oil, whisking vigorously. Set aside.

3. Drain the apples and pat them dry between layers of paper towels.

4. Arrange the greens down the center of a serving platter. Add the apples, dried cranberries, pistachios, and blue cheese on top. Drizzle evenly with the vinaigrette. Garnish with chives.

IDEA
If you are not a fan of Blue Cheese, you can substitute it with big cubes of a sharp Cheddar or Gruyère, opt for a creamier Goat Cheese, or even Brie! Adjust to your tastes with a cheese that balances the tartness of the apples and cranberries.

A THOUGHT
It is amazing how a few simple changes to ingredients can give you an entirely new flavor perspective! Instead of a heavy creamy dressing, I love this vinaigrette with apple cider vinegar, cinnamon, and honey. It is light and airy, but still gives a vinegary punch against the crisp apples and tart cranberries.

INGREDIENTS & PREP

Granny Smith Apple - 1, cored, thinly sliced into matchsticks

Lemon Juice - 1, freshly juiced

Apple Cider Vinegar - ¼ cup

Honey - ¼ cup

Cinnamon - ½ teaspoon

Sea Salt - ½ teaspoon

Black Pepper - ¼ teaspoon, freshly cracked

Olive Oil - 6 tablespoons

Spring Mix Greens - 4 ounces

Dried Cranberries - ¼ cup

Pistachios - ¼ cup

Blue Cheese - 2 ounces, crumbled (Roquefort recommended)

Chives - ¼ cup, cut into 1½-inch lengths

PLANNING
Yield - serves 2

NOTES

SOUPS & SALADS

Roasted Cauliflower Soup

A HEARTY SOUP DELICATELY ENHANCED WITH HERBES DE PROVENCE

DIRECTIONS

SOUP

1. Pre-heat the oven to 425 degrees F.

2. Place the cauliflower florets onto a sheet pan and toss with 4 tablespoons of olive oil, salt, and pepper. Roast for 25-30 minutes, until lightly browned and tender.

3. Meanwhile, in a medium Dutch oven or heavy-bottomed pan set over medium heat, add the butter and remaining 1 tablespoon of olive oil. Once hot, add the carrots and onions. Cook for 8-10 minutes, stirring occasionally until tender.

4. Add the garlic and Herbes de Provence and cook for another 1-2 minutes more, being careful not to burn the garlic.

5. Add the stock, raise the heat to high, and bring to a slow boil. Then, reduce the heat and simmer for 5 minutes. Turn off the heat.

6. Add the roasted cauliflower. Using an immersion blender or food processor, purée the soup until smooth and thick. Stir in the half & half. Reheat over medium heat until just heated through.

7. Garnish with green onions and croutons. Serve hot.

BUTTER CROUTONS

8. In a medium sauté pan set over medium heat, add the butter. Once melted, add the prepared bread cubes. Toast for 5-10 minutes, tossing occasionally, until lightly brown. Garnish the hot soup and serve.

INGREDIENTS & PREP

SOUP

Cauliflower – 1 head, just florets

Olive Oil – 5 tablespoons, divided

Sea Salt – ½ teaspoon

Black Pepper – ½ teaspoon, freshly cracked

Butter – 2 tablespoons, unsalted

Carrot – 1 medium, peeled, 1-inch diced

Yellow Onion – 1 small, 1-inch diced

Garlic – 2 cloves, finely minced

Herbes de Provence – ½ teaspoon, dried, lightly crushed

Vegetable Stock – 2½ cups

Half & Half – ½ cup

Scallions – 1 stalk, white and light green parts, trimmed, thinly sliced

BUTTER CROUTONS

French Boule – 2 slices, cut into ½-inch cubes

Butter – 3 tablespoons, unsalted

PLANNING

Bake – 25-30 minutes, at 425 degrees F

Yield – serves 2

FOOD FOR THOUGHT

Whenever I make homemade soups, I try to create a little unexpected twist when it comes to flavor. I do not want something that's just a "one note" flavorless soup, but instead something that is layered with flavors and perhaps even a little bit out of the ordinary. That is exactly what the dried blend of Herbes de Provence does in my *Roasted Cauliflower Soup*. It adds a classic savory note typically expected in soups, but also a little bit of a floral tone from the dried lavender that is a part of the herb blend. In the end, this soup is filled with layered aromatics, a fantastic texture, it is filling, and something you will be delighted to serve!

SOUPS & SALADS

Roasted Fruit *with* Rosemary Vinaigrette
A WARM SALAD WITH TRULY FABULOUS LAYERS OF FLAVOR!

DIRECTIONS

ROSEMARY VINAIGRETTE

1. In a small sauce pan set over medium heat, add the olive oil, honey, rosemary, and black peppercorns.

2. Bring to a simmer, then remove from the heat, cover, and allow to sit for 20 minutes.

3. Next, place a fine mesh sieve over a medium bowl. Strain the warm mixture, making sure to capture the peppercorns and rosemary in the sieve.

4. Lastly, whisk in the balsamic vinegar until full incorporated. Set aside.

ROASTED FRUIT

5. Start by pre-heating the oven to 450 degrees F.

6. Place all of the fruit onto a half sheet pan. Toss with olive oil, salt, and pepper.

7. Roast for 10-12 minutes, until the fruit just begins to release their juices. During the last 3 minutes, add the pecan halves to the fruit to toast.

ASSEMBLY

8. Arrange the greens onto a platter or a serving bowl. Evenly distribute the warm fruit, pecans, and crumbled Feta. Drizzle with vinaigrette.

9. Serve warm.

INGREDIENTS & PREP

Pecans – ¾ cup, whole halves

Spring Mix Greens – 3 ounces

French Feta – 5 ounces, crumbled

ROSEMARY VINAIGRETTE

Olive Oil – ¼ cup

Honey – ¼ cup

Rosemary – 1 sprig, fresh, about 4 inches

Whole Black Peppercorns – ¾ teaspoon

Balsamic Vinegar – 1 tablespoon

ROASTED FRUIT

Green Grapes – 1 cup, seedless

Red Grapes – 1 cup, seedless

Plums – 2, pitted, cut into quarters

Peaches – 2, pitted, cut into sixths

Olive Oil – 1 tablespoon

Sea Salt – ½ teaspoon

Black Pepper – ¼ teaspoon, freshly cracked

PLANNING

Bake – 10-12 minutes, at 450 degrees F

Yield – serves 2

NOTES

IDEA

My *Roasted Fruit with Rosemary Vinaigrette* salad is on the larger side and really can be made into an entrée when served after a heavier hors d'oeuvre like my **Baked Camembert with Pears & Maple**, page 89. This salad is especially wonderful when peaches or plums are not in season. Roasting them really brings out their flavors and makes them perfectly tender.

TABLE FOR TWO | 141

SOUPS & SALADS

Warm White Bean Salad
A LUSCIOUS AND SUBSTANTIAL SALAD BURSTING WITH RUSTIC CHARM!

DIRECTIONS

1. In a small sauce pan set over medium heat, add the olive oil, garlic, rosemary, thyme, and red pepper flakes. Cook until it just begins to simmer.

2. Then, remove the pan from the heat and add the white beans. Stir to coat the beans with the oil and herbs. Cover and set aside for 10 minutes.

3. Scatter the arugula across a platter or shallow bowl.

4. Remove the rosemary and thyme from the beans. Using a slotted spoon, spoon the beans onto the arugula. Evenly distribute the mozzarella, chives, Parmesan cheese, salt, and pepper.

5. Drizzle the warm olive oil over the top of the entire salad and serve.

INGREDIENTS & PREP

Olive Oil – ⅓ cup

Garlic – 2 cloves, thinly sliced

Rosemary – 2 small sprigs

Thyme – 4 sprigs

Red Pepper Flakes – ¼ teaspoon

Cannellini Beans – 1 can (15 ounces), drained, well rinsed

Arugula – 1 cup

Fresh Mozzarella – 4 ounces, fresh, torn into small pieces

Chives – 2 tablespoons, ¾-inch sliced on the diagonal

Parmesan Cheese – 3 tablespoons, freshly grated (Parmigiano-Reggiano recommended)

Sea Salt – ¾ teaspoon

Black Pepper – ½ teaspoon, freshly cracked

PLANNING

Yield – serves 2

FOOD FOR THOUGHT
White beans have such a velvety texture, especially when they are slightly warm and swimming in a robust flavored olive oil! This is one of my favorite salads – I love the way it all comes together with everyday ingredients, simply prepared and layered. The charm is really the earthy presentation – torn fresh mozzarella with rough edges, warm white beans, big spears of fresh chives, and a handful of peppery arugula, all of which are scattered beautifully on a big platter. Aside from this being a favorite salad, it also is one of the easiest salads I have ever made. You will be amazed at how flavorful and filling my *Warm White Bean Salad* is – perfect for entertaining!

NOTES

Sides

FABULOUS DISHES TO COMPLIMENT ANY MENU

Apple & Blue Cheese Slaw, 147

Balsamic Roasted Pearl Onions, 149

Brussels Sprouts with Strawberries, 151

Carpaccio of Cucumber, 153

Corn Gratin with White Cheddar, 155

Crème Fraîche Glazed Root Vegetables, 157

Dried Figs & Warm Orzo, 159

Herbes de Provence Tomatoes, 161

Roasted Cauliflower with Curried Browned Butter, 163

Triple Cream Sweet Potato Wedges, 165

Zucchini & Potato Gratin, 167

SIDES

Apple & Blue Cheese Slaw
A REFRESHINGLY CRISP AND TANGY INTERPRETATION OF AN OLD CLASSIC!

DIRECTIONS

DRESSING

1. Place all of the ingredients into a small bowl of a food processor fitted with a steel blade. Pulse until well mixed, but still chunky. Set aside.

SLAW

2. Place all of the ingredients into a medium bowl. Add the dressing and toss until everything is very well mixed.

3. Serve immediately, or chilled.

TIP
This recipe makes a slightly larger portion for two people. I think it actually tastes better the next day as it sits in the refrigerator allowing the flavors to meld and blend together.

A LITTLE STORY
It has taken me years and years to come to like (not even love!) slaw. To me, it was always gloopy and runny, and just tasteless - yuck! Well, times have changed and now I love certain flavor combinations of really complex and interesting slaws. Instead of tossing cabbage with just mayo, sour cream, and other ingredients, I thought it would be even better with a tangy blue cheese dressing, crisp granny smith apples, golden raisins, and lots of fresh herbs. This has become a staple at client dinner parties, as well as at my own dinner table!

INGREDIENTS & PREP

DRESSING

Mayonnaise - ¼ cup

Crème Fraîche - ¼ cup

Blue Cheese - 3½ ounces (Danish variety recommended)

Half & Half - 1 tablespoon

Garlic - 1 clove, crushed using a garlic press

Champagne Vinegar - 2 teaspoons

Sea Salt - ¼ teaspoon

Black Pepper - ¼ teaspoon

SLAW

Red Cabbage - 8 ounces, shredded

Golden Raisins - ¾ cup

Granny Smith Apple - 1 medium, ½-inch diced

Scallions - 2 tablespoons, white and light green parts, thinly sliced

Parsley - 2 tablespoons, fresh, finely minced (Italian flat leaf parsley recommended)

Basil - 1½ tablespoons, fresh, finely minced

Sea Salt - ½ teaspoon

Black Pepper - ¼ teaspoon, freshly cracked

PLANNING

Yield - serves 2

SIDES

Balsamic Roasted Pearl Onions
ONE OF MY ALL-TIME FAVORITE RECIPES FOR EASY AND ELEGANT ENTERTAINING

DIRECTIONS

① Pre-heat the oven to 450 degrees F. Line a small oven-proof dish with aluminum foil. Set aside.

② Fill a small pan half way with water and bring to a simmer. Drop in the whole pearl onions for 5 minutes, to help loosen their skins. Drain the onions.

③ Once cool enough to handle, and using a small knife, cut off the ends and peel each onion.

④ Add the peeled onions, olive oil, vinegar, salt, and pepper to the prepared dish. Toss to evenly coat.

⑤ Roast for 35-40 minutes, tossing 3 times during the cooking process, until the onions are tender and the vinegar has reduced to a think syrup.

⑥ Transfer to a serving dish and serve hot, or at room temperature.

INGREDIENTS & PREP

Golden Pearl Onions - 10 ounces, fresh

Olive Oil - 1 tablespoon

Balsamic Vinegar - 2 tablespoons

Sea Salt - ¼ teaspoon

Black Pepper - ¼ teaspoon, freshly cracked

PLANNING

Bake - 35-40 minutes, at 450 degrees F

Yield - serves 2

IDEA
Besides my *Balsamic Roasted Pearl Onions* being so incredibly simple to make, they can be served in a variety of very savvy ways. A few of my favorites are as part of a roasted vegetable platter, in a salad, as a side dish with my **Apple & Herb Wellington** (page 171) and green salad, or as part of cocktail hour alongside Roquefort cheese, slices of baguette, my **Spiced Chickpeas** (page 113), and other little nibbles. If you decide to serve as part of cocktail hour, have some small cocktail forks on hand so your guest can pick up each onion with ease.

FOOD FOR THOUGHT
There is something very satisfying about simple food that is less about the fuss and instead all about the flavor. From the ingredients, to the preparation, to the taste, some of the best-tasting dishes can be the simplest to make. My *Balsamic Roasted Pearl Onions* have only five ingredients, take hardly any real kitchen effort, and just roast away in the oven, giving your kitchen an aromatic hint of sweet onions and tangy vinegar, and a fabulously delicious dish to serve and enjoy.

NOTES

SIDES

Brussels Sprouts *with* Strawberries
A PERFECT BLEND OF SAVORY AND SWEET, WITH A BURST OF VINEGAR

DIRECTIONS

1. Pre-heat the oven to 425 degrees F.

2. Place the Brussels sprouts onto a half sheet pan. Toss with 1 tablespoon of olive oil, and ¼ teaspoon each of salt and pepper. Roast for 15-20 minutes, until tender and caramelized, tossing once during cooking.

3. Meanwhile, in a small sauté pan set over medium heat, add the remaining 2 tablespoons of olive oil. Once hot, add the red onion, and remaining ¼ teaspoon each of salt and pepper. Cook for 2-3 minutes, stirring occasionally, until the onions become soft, but not browned.

4. Then, add the garlic and strawberries and cook another 60 seconds.

5. Place the onions and strawberries in the center of a serving bowl. Add the roasted Brussels sprouts.

6. Drizzle everything with balsamic vinegar and then sprinkle with Parmesan cheese, fresh basil, and more freshly cracked black pepper. Serve.

INGREDIENTS & PREP

Brussels Sprouts – ½ pound, ends trimmed, cut in half

Olive Oil – 3 tablespoons, divided

Sea Salt – ½ teaspoon, divided

Black Pepper – ½ teaspoon, divided

Red Onion – ½ small onion, thinly sliced

Garlic – 2 cloves, finely minced

Strawberries – ½ pound, hulled, quartered

Balsamic Vinegar – 1½ tablespoons

Parmesan Cheese – 3 tablespoons, freshly grated (Parmigiano-Reggiano recommended)

Basil – 1½ tablespoons, fresh, roughly chopped

PLANNING

Bake – 15-20 minutes, at 425 degrees F

Yield – serves 2

A LITTLE STORY
I love recipes that combine interesting ingredients that normally would make people say, "Really?" I remember a time when I was testing French omelettes one evening a few years back and decided that I would try adding lemon zest, and Ryan kind of looked at me like, "Seriously, I am starving, don't ruin it with something weird!" Well, we did have omelettes brightened up with a lemony zing and they were incredibly delicious, and Ryan-approved! The combination of flavors, textures, and a surprise ingredient is, in my opinion, what often transforms a good recipe into a fabulous one! After you make my *Brussels Sprouts with Strawberries*, you will see (and taste!) exactly what I mean. These are just overflowing with complex flavors and even different textures. After I did the final test and photographed them, I ate *all* of the them myself, and without any regret!

NOTES

SIDES

Carpaccio *of* Cucumber
A VEGETARIAN VARIATION ON A MODERN ITALIAN SECONDO

DIRECTIONS

① In a small sauté pan set over medium heat, add the pine nuts. Toast for 5-6 minutes, tossing occasionally, until lightly golden brown.

② Select a large platter and start to arrange the cucumber slices, slightly overlapping each one, in a circular pattern, or another pattern that mimics the shape of your serving piece.

③ Evenly drizzle over the olive oil. Sprinkle with salt, pepper, dill, pine nuts, and Parmesan cheese.

④ Serve at room temperature.

INGREDIENTS & PREP

English Cucumber - 1 medium, very thinly sliced with a mandolin (or by hand)

Olive Oil - 2 tablespoons

Fleur de Sel - ¾ teaspoon

Black Pepper - ½ teaspoon

Dill - 1 teaspoon, fresh, roughly chopped

Pine Nuts - 2 tablespoons

Parmesan Cheese - ½ cup, freshly shaved then slightly crumbled (Parmigiano-Reggiano recommended)

PLANNING

Yield - serves 2

TIP
If you cannot find fresh dill, then try fresh basil or flat leaf parsley as these both can be wonderful herb variations for my *Carpaccio of Cucumber*!

IDEA
Besides serving this as a side dish, you can easily serve it as a salad course by individually plating each portion and then evenly dividing the ingredients per plate. Of course, this can also be enjoyed as an hors d'oeuvre. Having versatile recipes is the key to savvy entertaining!

A LITTLE STORY
When the incredibly chic and inspiring restaurant Fig & Olive opened in Chicago just a few blocks from our apartment, I ended up there every few days. They mesmerized me with their vegetarian dishes; the food was thoughtful, inspiring, and flavorful, not to mention incredibly beautiful. It wasn't until I was invited to a private dinner to celebrate the launch of chef and owner Laurent Halasz's cookbook (and got to meet his devastatingly elegant mother Francine!) that I fell even more in love with his chic eatery. Laurent and his family are so passionate about food and fresh ingredients, and to hear their story that evening is a moment I will never forget. This recipe is my take on a version from his book which uses zucchini, which is also delicious!

NOTES

SIDES

Corn Gratin *with* White Cheddar
CLASSIC COMFORT FOOD WITH A RICH AND ELEGANT UPDATE

DIRECTIONS

1. Pre-heat the oven to 375 degrees F. Butter a gratin dish or other small oven-proof dish, roughly 1½ quarts, and place it onto a half sheet pan lined with parchment paper. Set aside.

2. In the bowl of a food processor fitted with a steel blade, add 1 cup of the corn kernels, the egg, half & half, and flour. Pulse until mostly smooth and then transfer into a medium bowl.

3. Next, to the same medium bowl, add the remaining corn kernels, thyme, salt, pepper, ½ cup of White Cheddar, and 1 tablespoon of Parmesan. Stir until everything is well mixed.

4. Pour the mixture into the prepared baking dish. Evenly distribute over the top the remaining cheeses.

5. Bake for 25-30 minutes, or until the edges are nicely browned.

6. Allow to cool for 5 minutes before serving.

INGREDIENTS & PREP

Butter - 1 tablespoon, unsalted, at room temperature

Sweet Corn - 3 ears, kernels only

Egg - 1 extra-large, at room temperature

Half & Half - ⅔ cup

Flour - 1½ tablespoons

Thyme - ½ teaspoon, fresh, minced

Sea Salt - ½ teaspoon

Black Pepper - ½ teaspoon, freshly ground

White Cheddar - 1 cup, freshly grated, divided

Parmesan Cheese - 3 tablespoons, freshly grated (Parmigiano-Reggiano recommended)

PLANNING

Bake - 25-30 minutes, at 375 degrees F

Yield - serves 2

A LITTLE STORY
Ever since I was little, corn on the cob has been one of my favorite things to eat. I can remember my auntie bringing home big bags of fresh corn from the grocery store for a cookout, and nan would get the biggest pot ready with boiling water. The house always smelled so wonderfully when corn on the cob was cooking away – almost thick with starch! I was never a fan of anything barbequed – instead, I would eat five or more heavily buttered and salted ears of corn myself (ahhh, childhood!). There are still days, when corn is in season, when I will do just that. A classic corn gratin is usually made with mostly-puréed corn that is mixed with milk and spices. I have to say, I am not a fan of those sorts of dishes when there isn't any texture, as it can be like eating baby food – yuck! This recipe is filled with not only great texture from whole kernels, but also aromatic fresh thyme, White Cheddar cheese, and spicy Parmesan!

NOTES

SIDES

Crème Fraîche Glazed Root Vegetables
THE NEW WAY OF ROASTING ROOT VEGETABLES!

DIRECTIONS

1. Pre-heat the oven to 425 degrees F.

2. Place the carrots and parsnips onto a half sheet pan. Toss with olive oil, salt, and pepper. Roast for 15-20 minutes, tossing once during cooking, until lightly browned and tender.

3. Meanwhile, in a small bowl, whisk together the crème fraîche, half & half, Parmesan cheese, honey, shallots, garlic, and red pepper flakes. Set aside.

4. Remove the vegetables from the oven and, using a pastry brush, brush them with half of the crème fraîche mixture. Return the vegetables to the oven and roast another 3-5 minutes, until the milk solids in the crème fraîche begin to brown. Repeat this same process for the remaining half of the glaze.

5. Transfer the vegetables to a serving platter, add more salt and pepper to taste, and garnish with fresh parsley leaves. Serve immediately.

TIP
The earthiness of the carrots and parsnips are wonderfully enhanced with the brightness of the fresh parsley. If parsley is not your thing, fresh basil can be a fabulous substitute.

FOOD FOR THOUGHT
When you roast vegetables with a little bit of olive oil, salt, and pepper, their natural sugars caramelize and they develop deeper and richer flavor and intensity. Roasting vegetables to be "al dente" also enhances their texture, to be wonderfully creamy on the inside. Roasting is one of the simplest ways to dramatically enhance most vegetables! I have come across many recipes, both in print and online, that involve roasting chicken with a crème fraîche glaze. And while I do not eat meat, I wondered what would happen if I roasted hearty root vegetables, like carrots and parsnips, with a savory crème fraîche glaze? As I discovered, and share with you here, magic happens turning regular roasted root vegetables into the most delicious and creamy vegetables you will have ever had. The slight tang from the crème fraîche adds to the sweetness of the vegetables, and the browning of the milk solids creates incredibly well-balanced flavor!

INGREDIENTS & PREP

Carrots - 2 large, peeled, cut into 2-inch pieces

Parsnips - 2 large, peeled, cut into 2-inch pieces

Olive Oil - 2 tablespoons

Sea Salt - ½ teaspoon

Black Pepper - ½ teaspoon, freshly ground

Crème Fraîche - ⅓ cup

Half & Half - 1 teaspoon

Parmesan Cheese - 1 tablespoon, freshly grated (Parmigiano-Reggiano recommended)

Honey - ½ teaspoon

Shallot - 1 small, finely minced

Garlic - 1 clove, crushed using a garlic press

Red Pepper Flakes - ¼ teaspoon

Parsley - ¼ cup, fresh, whole leaves (Italian flat leaf parsley recommended)

PLANNING

Bake - 15-20 minutes, at 425 degrees F

Yield - serves 2

NOTES
_____
_____
_____
_____
_____
_____
_____
_____

SIDES

Dried Figs & Warm Orzo

A DAZZLING, CREAMY, AND WARM PASTA SIDE DISH

DIRECTIONS

1. In a medium bowl, add the freshly cooked warm pasta and each of the prepared ingredients. Stir until well mixed.

2. Serve warm.

Tip: This is a perfect dish to make at the very last minute. Once the orzo is done cooking, drain it, and immediately add the ingredients. The heat from the pasta will gently melt the crème fraîche and warm the dried figs enough to be perfectly moist and tender. Once the dish is mixed, it should be served right away.

TIP
While my *Dried Figs with Warm Orzo* is intended to be served warm, it is also quite delicious when served at room temperature. This is a fabulous dish if you want to serve it as part of a buffet, or even a picnic.

FOOD FOR THOUGHT
When most people think of orzo, a short-cut pasta in the shape of a grain of rice, they typically think of it in a cold salad, or something served at room temperature. My *Dried Figs with Warm Orzo* is served warm so that the dried figs get a little soft from the heat of the pasta. The rich tang of the crème fraîche is balanced with fresh herbs, dried oregano, lemon zest, and sweetness of the dried figs for a creamy full-bodied dish that can stand on its own.

INGREDIENTS & PREP

Orzo - 1 cup uncooked, cooked according to package directions, still warm

Dried Figs - 1 cup, stems removed, quartered (Black Mission variety recommended)

Olive Oil - 1 tablespoon

Sea Salt - ¾ teaspoon

Black Pepper - ¾ teaspoon

Crème Fraîche - ⅓ cup, at room temperature

Butter - 1 tablespoon, unsalted, at room temperature

Parmesan Cheese - ⅓ cup, freshly grated (Parmigiano-Reggiano recommended)

Lemon Zest - 1½ teaspoons, freshly zested

Parsley - 2 tablespoons, fresh, roughly chopped (Italian flat leaf parsley recommended)

Basil - 1 tablespoon, fresh, roughly chopped

Oregano - ½ teaspoon, dried, lightly crushed

PLANNING
Yield - serves 2

NOTES
_____
_____
_____
_____
_____
_____
_____

SIDES

Herbes *de* Provence Tomatoes

WARM TOMATOES BURST WITH FLAVOR WITH MY ALL-TIME FAVORITE DRIED HERB BLEND!

DIRECTIONS

① Pre-heat the broiler to high.

② Place the tomatoes in a single layer on a half sheet pan.

③ Set the tomatoes under the broiler for 2-3 minutes, until they begin to blister.

④ Remove them from the oven. Place the hot tomatoes onto a serving platter and drizzle with olive oil.

⑤ Evenly sprinkle them with Herbes de Provence, truffle salt, pepper, parsley, and Parmesan cheese. Drizzle over the lemon juice.

⑥ Serve warm or at room temperature.

INGREDIENTS & PREP

Roma Tomatoes - 4, sliced ½-inch thick

Olive Oil - 3 tablespoons

Herbes de Provence - ½ teaspoon, lightly crushed

Truffle Salt - ¾ teaspoon

Black Pepper - ¼ teaspoon

Parsley - 1 tablespoon, fresh, finely minced (Italian flat leaf parsley recommended)

Parmesan Cheese - ⅓ cup, freshly grated (Parmigiano-Reggiano recommended)

Lemon Juice - 1 tablespoon, freshly squeezed

PLANNING

Broiler - pre-heat to high

Yield - serves 2

IDEA
These robust tomatoes can also be used for a traditional Caprese Salad, with Buffalo Mozzarella and freshly chopped basil, for a flavorful twist on a classic!

FOOD FOR THOUGHT
I often use the dried spice blend Herbes de Provence when baking bread, making sauces, creating chocolate truffles, and even on my *Herbes de Provence Popcorn* (page 103), to present a savory and floral flavor – which I just adore! When you cut tomatoes, their interiors are like little sponges to be infused with whatever you dress them with. I love this recipe because of its simple preparation and over-the-top flavor – not to mention the subtle yet complex hit of truffle salt!

NOTES

SIDES

Roasted Cauliflower *with* Curried Browned Butter

AN IMPRESSIVE SIDE DISH BATHED IN LUXURIOUS BROWNED BUTTER

DIRECTIONS

1. Pre-heat the oven to 375 degrees F.

2. Start by cutting away the green leaves at the bottom of the cauliflower head. Using a small knife, carefully cut off and remove the stem and the tough core, being careful to keep the head and florets intact.

3. Transfer the entire head of cauliflower onto a half sheet pan and drizzle ¼ cup of olive oil on the entire head, including the underside where the core used to be. Sprinkle evenly with salt and pepper, including the underside. Place the head, core side down, onto the sheet pan and cover with aluminum foil. Roast for 30 minutes, until tender.

4. Meanwhile, in a small sauté pan set over medium-low heat, add the butter. Once it begins to melt, add the shallots, garlic, and red pepper flakes. Cook for 8-10 minutes, stirring occasionally, until the butter begins to turn a light amber color and the milk solids on the bottom of the pan turn brown.

5. Place a fine mesh sieve over a small bowl and carefully strain the hot butter into the bowl, catching and discarding the cooked garlic and shallots.

6. Whisk the curry powder into the strained butter and set aside.

7. After 30 minutes, remove the foil from the head of cauliflower, drizzle the remaining ¼ cup of olive oil over the top, and return to the oven to cook, uncovered, for another 35-45 minutes, until golden brown.

8. Next, using a spatula, transfer the entire roasted head of cauliflower into a shallow bowl or platter. Spoon over the curried brown butter, add more salt and pepper to taste, and garnish with fresh basil.

9. Serve immediately.

INGREDIENTS & PREP

Cauliflower - 1 head

Olive Oil - ½ cup, divided

Sea Salt - ¾ teaspoon

Black Pepper - ¾ teaspoon

Butter - 1 stick, unsalted, at room temperature

Shallot - 1 small, thinly sliced

Garlic - 2 cloves, thinly sliced

Red Pepper Flakes - ¼ teaspoon

Yellow Curry Powder - ¾ teaspoon

Basil - ¼ cup, fresh, julienned

PLANNING

Bake - 65-85 minutes, at 375 degrees F

Yield - serves 2

NOTES

SIDES

Triple Cream Sweet Potato Wedges
FAMILIAR FLAVORS, LAYERED TO SWEET AND SAVORY PERFECTION

DIRECTIONS

1. Pre-heat the oven to 450 degrees F.

2. In a small bowl, combine the rosemary and garlic. Set aside.

3. Cut each sweet potato in half lengthwise, and then cut each half into three long evenly-sized wedges.

4. Place the wedges onto a sheet pan and toss with olive oil. Arrange the potatoes in a single layer and sprinkle evenly with salt and pepper.

5. Roast for 20 minutes, and then turn each wedge with a spatula. Bake for another 5 minutes. Remove from the oven, sprinkle with the rosemary and garlic mixture, and bake for an addition 5 minutes.

6. Remove the sheet pan from the oven. Set the broiler to high.

7. Place the wedges into an oven-proof serving dish and evenly distribute the Brie pieces over the wedges.

8. Place the dish with the wedges under the broiler until the cheese is bubbly and melted, about 2-3 minutes.

9. Remove from the oven, sprinkle with basil, drizzle with honey, and more salt and pepper to taste. Serve immediately.

INGREDIENTS & PREP

Rosemary - 1 teaspoon, fresh, finely minced

Garlic - 3 cloves, finely minced

Sweet Potatoes - 2 medium, peeled

Olive Oil - 2 tablespoons

Sea Salt - ½ teaspoon

Black Pepper - ½ teaspoon, freshly cracked

Triple Cream Brie Cheese - 3½ ounces, chilled, thinly sliced, cut into ¾-inch pieces

Basil - ¼ cup, fresh, roughly chopped

Honey - 1 tablespoon

PLANNING

Bake - 30 minutes, at 450 degrees F

Broil - 2-3 minutes, set at high

Yield - serves 2

NOTES

_____
_____
_____
_____
_____
_____
_____
_____

TIP
Triple Cream Brie is a wonderfully luxurious cheese with such a creamy texture! If you cannot find Triple Cream, there are Double Cream varieties that are quite delicious as well. You can also use a standard Brie. Choose one that is very flavorful. Ask your cheesemonger for a sample to taste. Most grocery stores and cheese shops will happily oblige.

SIDES

Zucchini & Potato Gratin
A FABULOUS SIDE DISH, OR EVEN A MAIN COURSE WITH A GREEN SALAD!

DIRECTIONS

1. Start by pre-heating the oven to 400 degrees F. Butter a gratin dish, or other small dish, about 1½ quarts. Combine the salt, pepper, and thyme in a small bowl. Set both steps aside.

2. In a small sauce pan set over medium heat, add the heavy cream, butter, nutmeg, and lightly crushed garlic. Allow the mixture to come to a simmer, then add the flour and whisk rapidly to incorporate. Remove from the heat, cover, and allow to steep for 15 minutes.

3. Remove the whole garlic pieces with a slotted spoon and discard.

4. In the meantime, alternating between each of the three potatoes and the zucchini, arrange a layer on the bottom of your prepared dish, allowing each slice to overlap by about ½-inch. Sprinkle with a third of the salt, pepper, and thyme mixture, and a third of the Gruyère. Repeat this same step once more.

5. Next, arrange the final third layer of vegetables on top. Carefully pour the warm cream mixture over the vegetables.

6. Sprinkle the top with the remaining salt, pepper, thyme, and Gruyère.

7. Place onto a half sheet pan and bake for 30-35 minutes, or until the vegetables are tender, the top is browned, and the sides are bubbling.

8. Remove from the oven and allow to rest for 5 minutes before serving.

TIP
You can assemble this gratin up to two hours ahead of time and allow it to sit at room temperature. I would suggest baking right before you are ready to serve to savor the warm creamy texture fresh from the oven!

FOOD FOR THOUGHT
The word "gratin" comes from the French word gratinée, which means to brown, and typically uses breadcrumbs and/or cheese on the top to achieve a lovely golden color. This recipe really is unique as it has three varieties of potatoes and zucchini, all of which add their own flavors, and enhanced by fresh thyme!

INGREDIENTS & PREP

Sea Salt - ¾ teaspoon

Black Pepper - ¾ teaspoon

Thyme - 1 teaspoon, fresh, finely minced

Heavy Cream - ⅓ cup

Butter - 1 tablespoon, unsalted

Nutmeg - ⅛ teaspoon, freshly grated

Garlic - 3 cloves, lightly crushed

Flour - 2 teaspoons, all-purpose

Purple Potato - 1 medium, peeled, sliced ⅛-inch thick

Yukon Gold Potato - 1 medium, peeled, sliced ⅛-inch thick

Sweet Potato - 1 medium, peeled, sliced ⅛-inch thick

Zucchini - 1 medium, peeled, sliced ⅛-inch thick

Gruyère Cheese - ⅔ cup, freshly grated

PLANNING

Bake - 30-35 minutes, at 400 degrees F

Yield - serves 2

NOTES

Main Courses
PERFECTLY PORTIONED FOR YOU AND YOUR +1

Apple & Herb Wellington, 171

Butternut Squash Medallions with Wilted Spinach, 173

Caramelized Onion & White Cheddar Mac 'n Cheese, 175

Chicago Sliders, 177

Cinnamon Raisin Grilled Cheese, 179

Country Frittata with Petite Salad, 181

Fennel & Red Pepper Risotto, 183

French Lentils with Apples & Beets, 185

Herbed Cannellini Bean "Meatballs", 187

Hot & Sour Coconut Noodles, 189

Orange & Rosemary Cream Sauce, 191

Pear & Onion Tart, 193

Quinoa with Fresh Herbs, 195

Savory Dutch-Flan with Golden Potatoes, 197

Stove-Top Paella, 199

Sweet Potato Curry, 201

Truffled Toast with Asparagus, 203

Vegetable & Arugula Tacos, 205

Vietnamese-Inspired Pho, 207

MAIN COURSES

Apple & Herb Wellington

A MODERN VEGETARIAN VARIATION WRAPPED UP IN A CLASSIC FLAKY PASTRY CRUST!

DIRECTIONS

1. Start by pre-heating the oven to 400 degrees F. Line a half sheet pan with parchment paper. Set aside.

2. In a medium sauté pan set over medium heat, add the olive oil. Once hot, add the fennel, onion, parsnip, apples, thyme, salt, and pepper. Cook for 10-12 minutes, stirring occasionally, until very tender, but not browned.

3. Next, add the garlic and parsley and continue cooking for another 1 minute, being careful not to burn the garlic. Transfer to a medium bowl to cool for 5 minutes. Once cooled, stir in the cashews, raisins, and both cheeses.

4. Next, on a lightly floured surface, roll out the thawed puff pastry dough to a sheet roughly 12x14-inches. Cut the dough in half creating 2 pieces measuring 12x7-inches each.

5. Divide the filling in half and spoon each half evenly onto the bottom half of each piece of dough, leaving a ½-inch border around the edges. Brush the border with egg wash, and fold over the top half of the puff pastry to complete enclose the filling. Using the tines of a fork, seal the edges of the dough by pressing the tines lightly into the dough. Do this on all three sides or each packet. Transfer to the prepared baking sheet.

6. Brush the tops with egg wash. Using a small knife, cut three slits on the top of each packet (this allows steam to escape while baking).

7. Bake for 15-20 minutes, or until the pastry is puffed up and golden brown. Remove from the oven and allow to cool for 5 minutes before serving.

IDEA

I love the versatility of my *Apple & Herb Wellington*. You can change out the fresh herbs and filling and adapt it to take advantage of seasonal availability. During the fall and winter, I like to use fresh sage and rosemary and replace the parsnip with butternut squash. In the spring and summer, I enjoy basil and chives and replace the apple with zucchini. Once you feel comfortable with the simple technique for the pastry, have fun experimenting with different vegetables and herb combinations you enjoy – and remember to write down your variations the first time!

INGREDIENTS & PREP

Olive Oil - 3 tablespoons

Fennel - ¾ cup, ½-inch diced

Yellow Onion - 1 medium, ½-inch diced

Parsnip - 1 medium, peeled, ½-inch diced

Pink Lady Apple - 1 medium, ½-inch diced

Thyme - 2 teaspoons, fresh, finely minced

Sea Salt - ¾ teaspoon

Black Pepper - ¾ teaspoon

Garlic - 2 cloves, finely minced

Parsley - 3 tablespoons, fresh, finely minced (Italian flat leaf parsley recommended)

Raw Cashews - ⅓ cup, roughly chopped

Golden Raisins - ⅓ cup

Parmesan Cheese - 3 tablespoons, freshly grated (Parmigiano-Reggiano recommended)

Gruyère Cheese - 3 ounces, ¼-inch cubed

Frozen Puff Pastry - 1 sheet, thawed overnight in the refrigerator

Egg Wash - 1 extra-large egg lightly beaten with 1 tablespoon of water

PLANNING

Bake - 15-20 minutes, at 400 degrees F

Yield - serves 2

MAIN COURSES

Butternut Squash Medallions *with* Wilted Spinach
AN EASY-TO-MAKE DINNER WITH A TRÈS CHIC PRESENTATION!

DIRECTIONS

1. Pre-heat the oven to 425 degrees F.

2. Place the butternut squash medallions and leeks in a single layer onto a half sheet pan. Brush both sides of the vegetables with olive oil. Sprinkle the tops with salt and pepper.

3. Roast for 15 minutes. Then, carefully flip the vegetables, return to the oven, and continue roasting for another 7-10 minutes, or until the butternut squash is tender and the leeks are browned.

4. About 5 minutes before the vegetables are finished cooking, in a 10-inch sauté pan set over medium heat, add the French Bistro Vinaigrette. Once hot, add the spinach leaves and cook until wilted and tender, about 4-5 minutes.

5. Evenly divide the cooked spinach into the center of two diner plates. Remove the vegetables from the oven and place two butternut squash medallions onto the spinach on each plate, slightly overlapping. Then garnish the top of the medallions on each plate with a cooked leek half.

6. Sprinkle with Parmesan cheese and serve immediately.

INGREDIENTS & PREP

Butternut Squash – 1 small, peeled, cut in to 4 medallions ¾-inch thick

Leek – ½ large stalk, washed, trimmed, cut in half lengthwise

Olive Oil – 2 tablespoons

Sea Salt – ¼ teaspoon

Black Pepper – ¼ teaspoon

French Bistro Vinaigrette – 5 tablespoons (page 133)

Baby Spinach – 2 large handfuls, fresh

Parmesan Cheese – 2 tablespoons, freshly grated (Parmigiano-Reggiano recommended)

PLANNING

Bake – 25 minutes, at 425 degrees F

Yield – serves 2

TIP
For the butternut squash medallions, use the stem-end (or top portion) of the squash as that part does not have any seeds. You can use the remaining squash (and spinach) in my *Butternut Squash & Black Bean Soup* (page 131), and the remaining leek in my *Country Frittata with Petite Salad* (page 181).

FOOD FOR THOUGHT
I just love how très chic this recipe is – and it truly could not be easier! It is simply a few fresh vegetables and a "secret sauce", my *French Bistro Vinaigrette* (page 133). Because the vinaigrette already has both olive oil and vegetable oil already in it, it is perfect to sauté the fresh spinach and create a kind of "sauce." Then plating the roasted tender butternut squash and leeks creates a beautifully presented dinner for two, without undue fuss!

NOTES

MAIN COURSES

Caramelized Onion & White Cheddar Mac 'n Cheese
A FEW STEPS TRULY WORTH THE EFFORT FOR ELEGANT AND ELEVATED COMFORT

DIRECTIONS

1. Pre-heat the oven to 400 degrees F. Place two individual gratin dishes (6-7-inch diameter), or a small casserole dish, onto a half sheet pan. Set aside.

CARAMELIZED ONIONS

2. In a 10-inch sauté pan set over medium-low heat, add the olive oil and butter. Once hot, add the onions, sugar, salt, and pepper. Cook for 25-35 minutes, stirring occasionally, until the onions have turned a deep amber color and have caramelized.

3. Next, add the garlic and thyme. Cook for another 1-2 minutes, being careful not to burn the garlic. Transfer the onion mixture to a medium bowl using a slotted spoon, leaving behind most of the oil. Set aside.

TOPPING

4. In a small bowl, combine the panko and olive oil. Stir until well mixed. Set aside.

PASTA & CHEESE SAUCE

5. In a medium sauce pan set over medium heat, add the butter. Once hot, add the flour and cook for 2 minutes, whisking constantly.

6. Add the half & half, salt, and pepper. Continue cooking for another 2-3 minutes, whisking constantly, until the sauce thickens. Off the heat, whisk in both cheeses.

ASSEMBLY

7. Now, add the freshly cooked pasta and cheese sauce into the bowl with the onions. Stir until very well mixed.

8. Evenly divide the pasta into the gratin dishes and top each with half of the panko topping.

9. Bake for 5-7 minutes, or until the top is golden brown. Remove from the oven, garnish with fresh thyme sprigs, and serve immediately.

INGREDIENTS & PREP

CARAMELIZED ONIONS
Olive Oil – 3 tablespoons

Butter – 1 tablespoon, unsalted

Yellow Onion – 1 large, ½-inch diced

Sugar – 1 teaspoon, granulated

Sea Salt – ¼ teaspoon

Black Pepper – ¼ teaspoon, freshly cracked

Garlic – 2 cloves, finely minced

Thyme – 1 teaspoon, fresh, finely minced, plus extra sprigs for garnish

TOPPING
Panko Bread Flakes – ½ cup

Olive Oil – 2 tablespoons

PASTA & CHEESE SAUCE
Butter – 2 tablespoons

Flour – 1½ tablespoons

Half & Half – 1 cup, at room temperature

Sea Salt – ¼ teaspoon

Black Pepper – ¼ teaspoon

Fontina Cheese – ⅓ cup, freshly grated

White Cheddar Cheese – ¾ cup, freshly grated

Elbow Macaroni – 2 cups dried, cooked according to package directions for al dente

PLANNING
Bake – 5-7 minutes, at 400 degrees F

Yield – serves 2

MAIN COURSES

Chicago Sliders

INSPIRED BY THE ULTRA-FABULOUS HOTEL BARS OF CHICAGO

DIRECTIONS

FRESH THYME MAYO

1. Combine all of the prepared ingredients for the Fresh Thyme Mayo into a small bowl and mix until incorporated. Set aside.

CHICAGO SLIDERS

2. Start by pre-heating the oven to 350 degrees F. Line a half sheet pan with parchment paper. Place 1 tablespoon of olive oil into a small bowl. Set aside.

3. In the bowl of a small food processor fitted with a steel blade, add the drained beans, basil, and parsley. Pulse until the beans are almost smooth, but still have a bit of texture. Transfer to a medium bowl and set aside.

4. In a 10-inch sauté pan set over medium heat, add 2 tablespoons of olive oil and the butter. Once hot, add the red onions, thyme, rosemary, oregano, salt, pepper, and red pepper flakes. Cook for 5-7 minutes until the onions are soft, stirring occasionally. Next, add the garlic and cook for another 60 seconds, being careful not to burn the garlic.

5. Scrape the onion mixture and any remaining olive oil into the bean mixture. Add the bread crumbs, egg, half & half, and Parmesan cheese to the same bowl. Using a fork, combine all of the ingredients being careful not to compact the mixture.

6. Using a 2¼-inch scoop, form 6 balls by lightly rolling the mixture between the palms of your hands. Place each ball onto the prepared half sheet pan and bake for 10 minutes.

7. Next, using a spatula, gently flatten each ball into a patty about 1½-inches thick. Then brush the tops with the remaining 1 tablespoon of olive oil. Add the split buns, cut-side down, onto the same sheet pan to toast as the patties finish baking.

8. Return the half sheet pan to the oven and bake another 10-15 minutes, or until lightly browned.

ASSEMBLY

9. Assemble each slider with as much grated Gruyère and Fresh Thyme Mayo as desired. Serve hot.

INGREDIENTS & PREP

FRESH THYME MAYO

Mayonnaise - ¼ cup

Dijon Mustard - 1 teaspoon

Thyme - ½ teaspoon, fresh, finely minced

Lemon Zest - ½ teaspoon, freshly zested

Lemon Juice - 1 tablespoon, freshly squeezed

Sea Salt - ⅛ teaspoon

Black Pepper - ⅛ teaspoon, freshly cracked

CHICAGO SLIDERS

Cannellini Beans - 1 can (15 ounces), drained, rinsed

Basil - 3 tablespoons, fresh, finely minced

Parsley - 3 tablespoons, fresh, finely minced (Italian flat leaf parsley recommended)

Olive Oil - 3 tablespoons, divided

Butter - 1 tablespoon, unsalted

Red Onion - 1 small, ¼-inch diced

Thyme - 1 teaspoon, fresh, finely minced

Rosemary - 1 teaspoon, fresh, finely minced

Oregano - ¾ teaspoon, dried, lightly crushed

Sea Salt - ¾ teaspoon

Black Pepper - ¾ teaspoon

Red Pepper Flakes - ¼ teaspoon

Garlic - 3 cloves, finely minced

Dried Bread Crumbs - ⅓ cup, plus 1 tablespoon, plain variety

Egg - 1 extra-large, lightly beaten, at room temperature

Half & Half - 1 tablespoon

Parmesan Cheese - 3 tablespoons, freshly grated (Parmigiano-Reggiano recommended)

Pretzel Slider Buns - 6, split

Gruyère Cheese - ¾ cup, freshly grated, for topping

PLANNING

Bake - 20-25 minutes, at 350 degrees F

Yield - makes 6 vegetarian sliders

MAIN COURSES

Cinnamon Raisin Grilled Cheese
A COMFORT-FOOD DISH INSPIRED BY SAKS FIFTH AVENUE

DIRECTIONS

CREAMY FIG & THYME DRESSING

1. Combine all of the prepared ingredients in a small bowl and whisk until smooth. Set aside.

GRILLED CHEESE & PETITE SALAD

2. Spread 1 tablespoon of butter on one side of each slice of bread. Spread 1 tablespoon of fig preserves on the other side of each slice of bread.

3. Place two slices of bread, buttered side down, into the hot pan. Layer two slices of Brie on the preserves side facing up, and a generous layer of apples, and ¼ teaspoon of both salt and pepper. Top with the remaining two slices of bread, buttered sides up.

4. Toast each side for 5-7 minutes, or until golden brown and crisp.

5. Remove the sandwiches from the pan, cut on the diagonal, and arrange onto plates. Place a handful of greens onto each plate, drizzle with dressing, and serve.

INGREDIENTS & PREP

CREAMY FIG & THYME DRESSING

Fig Preserves - 2 tablespoons

Thyme - ¾ teaspoon, fresh, finely minced

Sea Salt - ½ teaspoon

Black Pepper - ½ teaspoon, freshly cracked

Olive Oil - 1 tablespoon

Crème Fraîche - 1 tablespoon

Parmesan Cheese - 1 tablespoon, freshly grated (Parmigiano-Reggiano recommended)

Half & Half - 2 tablespoons

GRILLED CHEESE & PETITE SALAD

Cinnamon Raisin Bread - 4 slices

Butter - 4 tablespoons, unsalted, at room temperature, divided

Fig Preserves - 4 tablespoons, divided

Triple Cream Brie Cheese - 5 ounces, thinly sliced, at room temperature

Granny Smith Apple - 1 small, thinly sliced

Sea Salt - ½ teaspoon, divided

Black Pepper - ½ teaspoon, divided

Spring Mix Greens - 4 ounces, divided

Dried Figs - for garnish (Black Mission variety recommended)

PLANNING

Yield - serves 2

A LITTLE STORY

Whenever there is a grilled cheese on a menu, chances are that I will order it. I came across an incredibly complex, yet delicate, grilled cheese at Sophie's at Saks in my neighborhood in Chicago. Sometimes I may need to "adjust" the ingredients in a grilled cheese sandwich to make it vegetarian – but in this case, everything was just perfect, and an inspiration for me to create my own variation of an elevated grilled cheese sandwich! Needless to say, I have served my *Cinnamon Raisin Grilled Cheese* at some of my "fancy-schmancy" dinner parties – and guests go crazy! Basic ingredients get a serious upgrade, done perfectly for two!

MAIN COURSES

Country Frittata *with* Petite Salad

INSPIRED BY FRESH INGREDIENTS AND BRIGHT FLAVORS

DIRECTIONS

1. Pre-heat the oven to 375 degrees F.

PETITE SALAD

2. In a small bowl, add the lemon zest, lemon juice, honey, mustard, salt, and pepper. Whisk until blended.

3. While continuing to whisk vigorously, slowly drizzle in both oils until the vinaigrette has emulsified. Set aside.

FRITTATA

4. In a large bowl, add the eggs, half & half, chives, parsley, Gruyère, and Pecorino. Whisk until the yolks and whites are fully blended. Set aside.

5. In a 10-inch oven-proof sauté pan set over medium heat, add the olive oil and butter. Once hot, add the leeks, asparagus, rosemary, thyme, salt, and pepper. Cook for 6-8 minutes until the leeks are tender, stirring occasionally. Add the garlic and tomatoes and cook for just another 30 seconds, being careful not to burn the garlic.

6. Next, add the egg mixture. Stir to make sure all of the ingredients in the pan are well distributed. Continue cooking for just about 1-2 minutes, until the edges just start to set.

7. Transfer the pan to the oven and bake for 12-15 minutes, or until the edges are lightly brown and the center of the frittata is just set. Do not over-bake the eggs or they will get tough and dry. Remove the pan from the oven and allow to rest for 5 minutes. They will continue to cook as it rests.

ASSEMBLY

8. In a medium bowl, add the arugula. Toss with enough of the vinaigrette to coat the leaves.

9. Pile the dressed arugula onto the frittata and serve from the pan.

INGREDIENTS & PREP

PETITE SALAD
Lemon Zest – ½ teaspoon, freshly zested
Lemon Juice – 2 tablespoons, freshly squeezed
Honey – ¾ teaspoon
Dijon Mustard – ½ teaspoon
Sea Salt – ¼ teaspoon
Black Pepper – ¼ teaspoon
Olive Oil – 1 tablespoon
Canola Oil – 3 tablespoons

FRITTATA
Eggs – 6 extra-large, at room temperature
Half & Half – 1 tablespoon
Chives – 2 tablespoons, fresh, roughly chopped
Parsley – 2 tablespoons, fresh, roughly chopped (Italian flat leaf parsley recommended)
Gruyère Cheese – ½ cup, freshly grated
Pecorino Cheese – 2 tablespoons, freshly grated
Olive Oil – 2 tablespoons
Butter – 1 tablespoon
Leeks – ½ large leek, washed, trimmed, ½-inch diced
Asparagus – 5 stalks, bottom ends trimmed and discarded, cut into ¾-inch lengths, tips included
Rosemary – ½ teaspoon, fresh, finely minced
Thyme – ½ teaspoon, fresh, finely minced
Sea Salt – ½ teaspoon
Black Pepper – ½ teaspoon
Garlic – 2 cloves, finely minced
Grape Tomatoes – 1 cup, whole
Arugula – 1 large handful, fresh

PLANNING
Bake – 12-15 minutes, at 375 degrees F
Yield – serves 2

MAIN COURSES

Fennel & Red Pepper Risotto

AN ELEGANT DISH FOR A SPECIAL OCCASION, OR EVEN A SIMPLE WEEKNIGHT MEAL!

DIRECTIONS

1. In a small Dutch oven set over medium heat, add the butter and olive oil. Once hot, add the red peppers, fennel, salt, and pepper. Cook for 7-9 minutes until tender, stirring occasionally.

2. Add the shallots, garlic, and Arborio rice and cook for another 2-3 minutes, until lightly toasted, stirring constantly.

3. Next, pour in the hot stock and bring to a boil. Then reduce the heat to low, cover, and simmer for 18-20 minutes, stirring occasionally.

4. Once almost all of the liquid is absorbed by the rice, turn off the heat and stir in the Parmesan cheese, Gorgonzola cheese, heavy cream, parsley, and lemon zest.

5. Serve immediately.

IDEA
If you do not have a small Dutch oven, any 10-inch skillet with a tight fitting lid will work well.

FOOD FOR THOUGHT
Risotto is one of my favorite comfort foods, and is probably one of the most versatile things you can make at home. The base is always Arborio rice—an Italian short grain rice with a creamy and chewy texture—and brought to life with stock and other fresh ingredients. If in your pantry you have Arborio rice, fresh herbs, left over vegetables (raw or cooked), and a bit of stock or broth, then an easy and cozy dinner can be ready in under 30 minutes (I love that!). My *Fennel & Red Pepper Risotto* really gets its depth of flavor from fennel and spicy Gorgonzola cheese – two very Italian ingredients, perfect for this elegant main course!

INGREDIENTS & PREP

Butter – 1 tablespoon, unsalted

Olive Oil – 2 tablespoons

Red Pepper – 1 medium, seeded, ½-inch diced

Fennel – 1½ cups, stalks and core removed and discarded, ½-inch diced

Sea Salt – ¼ teaspoon

Black Pepper – ½ teaspoon

Shallot – 1 large, finely minced

Garlic – 2 cloves, finely minced

Italian Arborio Rice – ½ cup

Vegetable Stock – 1½ cups, heated to barely simmering

Parmesan Cheese – ¼ cup, freshly grated (Parmigiano-Reggiano recommended)

Gorgonzola Cheese – ¼ cup, crumbled (piquant variety)

Heavy Cream – 1 tablespoon

Parsley – 2 tablespoons, fresh, finely minced (Italian flat leaf parsley recommended)

Lemon Zest – ½ teaspoon, freshly zested

PLANNING

Yield – serves 2

NOTES

MAIN COURSES

French Lentils *with* Apples & Beets

FABULOUS FOR ENTERTAINING, SERVED HOT, WARM, OR EVEN ROOM TEMPERATURE

DIRECTIONS

1. Start by placing the rinsed lentils, water, and bay leaf in a medium sauce pan set over high heat. Bring to just under the boiling point, then reduce the heat to low, and barely simmer for 20-30 minutes, stirring occasionally, until the lentil are no longer crunchy but still have a bite to them.

2. Meanwhile, in a 10-inch sauce pan set over medium heat, add the olive oil. Once hot, add the apple, carrot, salt, and pepper. Cook for 5-7 minutes, until the carrots are tender, stirring occasionally.

3. Add the garlic and shallots and continue cooking for another 1 minute, being careful not to burn the garlic.

4. Transfer to a medium bowl. Stir in the beets, basil, parsley, dill, and Parmesan cheese.

5. Once the lentils are finished cooking, drain any excess water, discard the bay leaf, and add the cooked lentils to the same bowl with the apple mixture. Add the lemon juice and stir to evenly combine. Serve.

TIP
For such a small number of beets, rather than going through the hassle of cooking and peeling them, I found that buying pre-cooked beets that have been steamed and peeled (either in the freezer or refrigeration section at my grocery store) was much easier. Even better, I really could not tell the difference whether they were freshly cooked or store-bought. You can also find them canned or in jars—just make sure they are not packed in a vinaigrette.

IDEA
French lentils have such earthy flavor and when paired with beets, fresh herbs, and a punch of lemon, they suddenly turn into a very elegant dish perfect as a main course. You can easily make this dish in advance and allow it to sit at room temperature for up to 2 hours.

INGREDIENTS & PREP

Green French Lentils – ¾ cup, very well rinsed, drained

Water – 2 cups

Bay Leaf – 1, dried or fresh

Olive Oil – 3 tablespoons

Granny Smith Apple – 1 medium, core removed and discarded, ½-inch diced

Carrot – 1 medium, peeled, ½-inch diced

Sea Salt – ½ teaspoon

Black Pepper – ½ teaspoon

Garlic – 2 cloves, finely minced

Shallot – 1 large, ¼-inch diced

Beets – 8 ounces, pre-cooked, peeled, ½-inch diced

Basil – 1 tablespoon, finely minced

Parsley – 1 tablespoon, fresh, finely minced (Italian flat leaf parsley recommended)

Dill – 1 tablespoon, finely minced

Parmesan Cheese – 4 tablespoons, freshly grated (Parmigiano-Reggiano recommended)

Lemon Juice – 1 tablespoon, freshly squeezed

PLANNING

Yield – serves 2

NOTES

MAIN COURSES

Herbed Cannellini Bean "Meatballs"

"MEATBALL" IS NOW A UNIVERSAL NOUN WITH THIS AS A REAL VEGETARIAN OPTION!

DIRECTIONS

1. Start by pre-heating the oven to 350 degrees F. Line a half sheet pan with parchment paper. Set aside.

2. In the bowl of a small food processor fitted with a steel blade, add the drained beans, basil, and parsley. Pulse until the beans are almost smooth, but still have a bit of texture. Transfer to a medium bowl and set aside.

3. In a 10-inch sauté pan set over medium heat, add the olive oil and butter. Once hot, add the red onions, thyme, rosemary, oregano, salt, pepper, and red pepper flakes. Cook for 5-7 minutes until the onions are soft, stirring occasionally.

4. Next, add the garlic and cook for another 1 minute, being careful not to burn the garlic.

5. Scrape the onion mixture and any remaining olive oil into the bean mixture. Add the bread crumbs, egg, half & half, and Parmesan cheese to the same bowl. Using a fork, combine all of the ingredients being careful not to compact the mixture.

6. Form each ball by lightly rolling 2 tablespoons of the mixture in the palms of your hands. Place each ball onto the prepared sheet pan, spaced evenly.

7. Bake for 20-25 minutes, until lightly browned and firm to the touch.

8. Remove from the oven and allow to rest for 3 minutes before removing them from the sheet pan. Serve hot.

INGREDIENTS & PREP

Cannellini Beans - 1 can (15 ounces), rinsed, drained

Basil - 3 tablespoons, fresh, finely minced

Parsley - 3 tablespoons, fresh, finely minced (Italian flat leaf parsley recommended)

Olive Oil - 2 tablespoons

Butter - 1 tablespoon, unsalted

Red Onion - 1 small, ¼-inch diced

Thyme - 1 teaspoon, fresh, finely minced

Rosemary - 1 teaspoon, fresh, finely minced

Oregano - ¾ teaspoon, dried, lightly crushed

Sea Salt - ¾ teaspoon

Black Pepper - ¾ teaspoon, freshly cracked

Red Pepper Flakes - ¼ teaspoon

Garlic - 3 cloves, finely minced

Dried Bread Crumbs - ⅓ cup, plus 1 tablespoon (plain variety)

Egg - 1 extra-large, lightly beaten, at room temperature

Half & Half - 1 tablespoon

Parmesan Cheese - 3 tablespoons, freshly grated (Parmigiano-Reggiano recommended)

PLANNING

Bake - 20-25 minutes, at 350 degrees F

Yield - makes 12 vegetarian meatballs

FOOD FOR THOUGHT

My *Herbed Cannellini Bean "Meatballs"* are incredibly flavorful, substantial, and have a fantastic texture. However, they are not intended to simmer or stew in a pot of sauce—they would fall apart as they are intended to be tender and not overly-dense. To showcase them best, time the baking of the "meatballs" for them to come out of the oven when you are ready to serve, and nestle them in your pasta that has already been dressed and tossed with your favorite sauce. For a fabulous hors d'oeuvre, you can also spoon your favorite sauce into gratin dishes, sans pasta, nestle in the "meatballs," top with cheese, and a few seconds under a broiler!

MAIN COURSES

Hot & Sour Coconut Noodles
GET READY TO CRAVE THESE NOODLES ALL THE TIME!

DIRECTIONS

① Place the diced avocados in a small bowl. Toss with lime juice and lime zest. Set aside.

② In a 10-inch sauté pan set over medium heat, add the butter and olive oil. Once hot, add the garlic, red pepper flakes, salt, and pepper. Cook for just 1 minute, being careful not to burn the garlic.

③ Add the coconut milk and Thai chili garlic paste, and raise the heat to high and bring to a boil, then reduce the heat and simmer for 3 minutes. Remove from the heat.

④ Once the fettuccini is cooked to al dente, and off the heat, add them to the coconut milk and toss to evenly coat.

⑤ Stir in the basil, green onions, and avocados, including the lime juice and zest.

⑥ Ladle everything into serving bowls and garnish with wasabi peas.

⑦ Serve immediately.

TIP
You can also make this with Japanese udon noodles, ramen noodles, or even linguini! Choose a noodle or pasta that has good texture when cooked and is on the thicker side.

A LITTLE STORY
No, seriously! I crave these noodles at least once a week! I have been making a variation of this dish for Ryan for years, especially when time is short but we still want a very satisfying dinner. Practice the few steps here and it can take only about 10 minutes from start to finish! If you allow the coconut milk to reduce for just a few minutes longer than what I have directed in this recipe, it becomes more of a thick cream sauce – both options are equally delicious. Thus turning it into a wonderfully complex and hearty dish loaded with fresh lime zest, creamy avocado, and spicy chili paste! Don't let the heat from the chili paste and red pepper flakes scare you, the acidity of the lime, in addition to the freshness of the herbs, helps balance the heat. Get ready for the cravings to begin!

INGREDIENTS & PREP

Fettuccini – 5 ounces, dried, cooked to package directions for al dente

Avocado – 2 medium, peeled, diced ¾-inch (Haas variety recommended)

Lime – 2 medium, zested, juiced

Butter – 1 tablespoon, unsalted

Olive Oil – 1 tablespoon

Garlic – 3 cloves, thinly sliced

Red Pepper Flakes – 1 teaspoon

Sea Salt – ¾ teaspoon

Black Pepper – ½ teaspoon, freshly cracked

Coconut Milk – 1 can (15 ounces)

Thai Chili Garlic Paste – ¾ teaspoon

Basil – ⅓ cup, fresh, roughly chopped

Scallions – ⅓ cup, thinly sliced

Wasabi Peas – for garnish

PLANNING

Yield – serves 2

NOTES

MAIN COURSES

Orange & Rosemary Cream Sauce

AN UNLIKELY COMBINATION OF INGREDIENTS THAT WILL EXCITE YOUR TASTE BUDS!

DIRECTIONS

1. In a 10-inch sauté pan set over medium heat, add the butter and olive oil. Once hot, add the red onions, salt, black pepper, and red pepper flakes. Cook for 5-7 minutes, stirring occasionally, until the onions are soft.

2. Next, add the rosemary, orange zest, and garlic. Cook for another 1 minute, being careful not to burn the garlic.

3. Lastly, reduce the heat to low, and add the olives and all three cheeses. Stir until just melted.

4. Serve immediately.

TIP
This is such a unique sauce, but is amazingly versatile with pasta, lasagna, over roasted vegetables, and even just for dipping big hunks of crusty bread! My particular favorite (shown) is over al dente bucatini pasta with chives and a very crisp, very chilled white wine.

IDEA
Cerignola olives are usually found in the deli or cheese section at most grocery stores. They are not pitted, so a little prep is needed, but very much worth the effort in the flavor gained from this variety of fresh olives. Use a small paring knife to slice down the sides of the olive against the pit, pull apart along the cut, and remove the pit from the flesh of the olive. It only takes a few minutes, and you'll be glad you took the time!

A LITTLE STORY
I love a dish that is both rustic and chic, not only in its presentation, but also in the way rich flavors layer with amazing textures. This dish, which has a very eclectic combination of ingredients, brings to mind a dish you would find in a quaint Italian village restaurant in the countryside that they have been making for a hundred years and everyone just knows that orange and rosemary belong together. Filled with fresh orange zest, rosemary, three different cheeses, and even Cerignola olives, my adventurous *Orange & Rosemary Cream Sauce* will awaken your taste buds with fantastic flavor, sure to satisfy even the most discerning palettes!

INGREDIENTS & PREP

Butter - 1 tablespoon, unsalted

Olive Oil - 1 tablespoon

Red Onion - ½ of a small onion, ¼-inch diced

Sea Salt - ½ teaspoon

Black Pepper - ½ teaspoon, freshly cracked

Red Pepper Flakes - ¼ teaspoon

Rosemary - ½ teaspoon, fresh, finely minced

Orange Zest - 1 teaspoon, freshly zested

Garlic - 2 cloves, finely minced

Cerignola Olives - ⅓ cup, ¼-inch diced

Mascarpone Cheese - 8 ounces

Goat Cheese - 3 ounces

Parmesan Cheese - 3 tablespoons, freshly grated (Parmigiano-Reggiano recommended)

PLANNING

Yield - serves 2

NOTES

_____

_____

_____

_____

_____

_____

_____

MAIN COURSES

Pear & Onion Tart

FROZEN PUFF PASTRY IS TRANSFORMED INTO A CRISPY ELEGANT TART!

DIRECTIONS

1. Pre-heat the oven to 400 degrees F. Line a half sheet pan with parchment paper. Set aside.

2. On a lightly floured work surface, roll out the thawed puff pastry sheet to be about a 10x10-inch square. Transfer it to the middle of the prepared sheet pan.

3. With a fork, prick the dough all over (evenly and close together), leaving a ¾-inch border. This will prevent the dough from puffing up and will create the flat bottom of the tart. Where the dough isn't pricked, it will puff up and create a "crust."

4. Arrange the slices of pears on the dough in straight rows, slightly overlapping each slice by ½-inch. Repeat this process until the entire surface of the dough is covered, except the "crust" border.

5. Next, evenly scatter the sliced onions onto the layer of pears.

6. Finally, distribute the cheese, drizzle with olive oil and honey, and sprinkle with salt and pepper. Brush the "crust" border with egg wash.

7. Bake for 25-30 minutes, or until the dough is puffed up and golden, and the cheese is starting to bubble and brown.

8. Remove the tart from the oven, sprinkle over the torn basil leaves and drizzle on the balsamic reduction. Serve immediately.

FOOD FOR THOUGHT

Most grocery stores now carry bottled balsamic vinegar reductions where the olive oils are stocked. If you can't find a reduction, use a really thick and syrupy balsamic vinegar.

Port Salut Cheese is a semi-soft pasteurized cow's milk cheese from Pays de la Loire, France – it has a distinctive orange rind and a mild flavor. Its creamy texture melts perfectly when baked. If you cannot find Port Salut, try for something similar, like a soft Gouda.

INGREDIENTS & PREP

Frozen Puff Pastry – 1 sheet, thawed in the refrigerator overnight

Bartlett Pear – 1 medium, cored, very thinly sliced

Yellow Onion – ½ small, very thinly sliced

Port Salut Cheese – 3 ounces, cut into ¾-inch pieces

Olive Oil – 2 tablespoons

Honey – 2 teaspoons

Fleur de Sel – ½ teaspoon

Black Pepper – ½ teaspoon, freshly cracked

Egg Wash – 1 extra-large egg lightly beaten with 1 tablespoon of water

Basil – ¼ cup, fresh, torn leaves

Balsamic Vinegar Reduction – 1 tablespoon (a good store-bought brand)

PLANNING

Bake - 25-30 minutes, at 400 degrees F

Yield - serves 2

NOTES

MAIN COURSES

Quinoa *with* Fresh Herbs

A PERFECTLY VERSATILE DISH, SERVED WARM OR ROOM TEMPERATURE

DIRECTIONS

1. Once the quinoa is cooked, drain any excess water and transfer the quinoa to a medium bowl.

2. While the quinoa is still hot, add the remaining ingredients, excluding the arugula. Stir until everything is well mixed.

3. Place handfuls of arugula in the center of two dinner plates or one big pile into the center of a serving bowl. Top the arugula with the warm quinoa.

4. Garnish with more Parmesan cheese and serve either warm or at room temperature.

TIP
This is also a wonderful entrée salad when served with the addition of crumbled goat cheese. And, if you don't care for black beans, white beans are a fabulous alternative!

IDEA
My *Quinoa with Fresh Herbs* salad develops its flavors the longer it sits. Allow to sit at room temperature for 30 minutes (if you have the time) before serving. Cover it tightly with plastic wrap to keep it warm. You can also make this in advance and store it in the refrigerator for up to two days, covered with plastic wrap. Allow it to sit at room temperature for at least 1 hour before serving. You may want to stir in an additional tablespoon of olive oil and crème fraîche to enhance its creamy texture.

FOOD FOR THOUGHT
When I am developing a new salad recipe, which has the possibility of endless flavor combinations, I start by first making a list of ingredients that I think would complement one another in a dish. Things like orange and basil, pear and parsley, lemon and thyme, rosemary and apples - you get it! Quinoa has a very earthy flavor and texture and really absorbs the flavors of whatever you mix with it, especially when it is warm. The crème fraîche and olive oil add such velvety body to the cooked quinoa helping to make this a fabulous main course!

INGREDIENTS & PREP

Quinoa - ¾ cup dry, cooked to package directions

Black Beans - 1 can (15 ounces), drained, rinsed

Bartlett Pear - 1 medium, cored, ½-inch diced

Orange - 1 medium, zested, peeled and white pith removed, ½-inch diced

Basil - 2 tablespoons, fresh, finely minced

Chives - 2 tablespoons, fresh, finely minced

Parsley - 2 tablespoons, fresh, finely minced (Italian flat leaf parsley recommended)

Shallot - 1 small, finely minced

Garlic - 2 cloves, crushed with a garlic press

Olive Oil - 3 tablespoons

Sea Salt - 1 teaspoon

Black Pepper - 1 teaspoon, freshly cracked

Crème Fraîche - 2 tablespoons

Parmesan Cheese - 3 tablespoons, plus more for garnish, freshly grated (Parmigiano-Reggiano recommended)

Arugula - 2 large handfuls, for serving

PLANNING

Yield - serves 2

MAIN COURSES

Savory Dutch-Flan *with* Golden Potatoes
MY UPDATED BREAKFAST DISH GETS A SAVORY MAIN COURSE MAKEOVER

DIRECTIONS

① Pre-heat the oven to 425 degrees F. Line a small plate with paper towels. Set aside.

POTATOES

② In a 10-inch sauté pan set over medium heat, add the olive oil and butter. Once hot, add the potatoes, salt, and pepper. Cook for 10-12 minutes, tossing occasionally, until golden brown.

③ Next, add the shallots and garlic. Cook for another 1 minute, being careful not to burn the garlic. Using a slotted spoon, transfer the potatoes to the prepared plate. Set aside.

DUTCH-FLAN

④ In a glass measuring cup, combine the milk, eggs, flour, salt, pepper, and thyme leaves. Whisk together until the batter is smooth. Set aside.

⑤ Place 2 individual gratin dishes (6-7 inches in diameter) onto a sheet pan. Place 1 tablespoon of butter into each dish. Place the sheet pan with the gratin dishes into the oven for 3 minutes.

⑥ Next, carefully remove the sheet pan from the oven and immediately divide the batter between the two hot gratin dishes (each should hold 1 cup of batter).

⑦ Return the sheet pan with the filled gratin dishes to the oven and bake for 14-15 minutes, or until the sides are puffed up and golden.

ASSEMBLY

⑧ Remove from the oven, and top each Dutch-Flan evenly with potatoes, cheese, and green onions. Serve immediately.

TIP
This is the same base as my *Banana & Maple Dutch-Flan* (page 65), but with the vanilla and honey traded for black pepper and fresh thyme. For more variations: Top each Dutch-Flan with caramelized onions and Blue cheese, or with sautéed asparagus and Gruyère cheese. Or, simply fresh diced tomatoes and basil!

INGREDIENTS & PREP
POTATOES
Olive Oil - 3 tablespoons

Butter - 1 tablespoon

Yukon Gold Potato - 1 large, ½-inch diced

Sea Salt - ¼ teaspoon

Black Pepper - ¼ teaspoon

Shallot - 1 small, finely minced

Garlic - 2 cloves, finely minced

DUTCH-FLAN
Whole Milk - ¾ cup, at room temperature

Eggs - 3 extra-large, at room temperature

Flour - ¾ cup, all purpose

Sea Salt - ¼ teaspoon

Black Pepper - ¼ teaspoon

Thyme - ¾ teaspoon, fresh, whole leaves

Butter - 2 tablespoons, unsalted, at room temperature

Pepper Jack Cheese - ½ cup, freshly grated, at room temperature

Scallions - 2 tablespoons, white and light green parts, thinly sliced

PLANNING
Bake - 14-15 minutes, at 425 degrees F

Yield - serves 2

NOTES
_____
_____
_____
_____
_____

MAIN COURSES

Stove-Top Paella

SAFFRON THREADS ADD INTENSE FLAVOR TO ONE OF MY MOST-REQUESTED RECIPES!

DIRECTIONS

1. In a small bowl, add the hot tap water and saffron threads. Set aside.

2. In a 10-inch sauté pan set over medium heat, add the olive oil. Once hot, add the orange and yellow peppers, red onion, and eggplant. Cook for 8-10 minutes, until the eggplant is tender, stirring occasionally.

3. Add the garlic, rice, and tomato paste. Continue cooking for another 1 minute, stirring constantly.

4. Next, add ½ teaspoon of lemon zest and white wine. Allow the liquid to reduce by half, about 1 minute, stirring constantly.

5. Add the saffron threads and water, vegetable stock, salt, pepper, paprika, and tomatoes. Raise the heat to high and bring to just under the boiling point. Then, immediately reduce the heat to low and simmer, covered, for 20-25 minutes, stirring every 5 minutes, until most of the liquid is absorbed and the rice is cooked, but not mushy.

6. Lastly, off the heat, stir in the peas, capers, green onions, and parsley. Cover and let stand for another 5 minutes for all of the flavors to blend.

7. Stir in the remaining ½ teaspoon of lemon zest and serve.

FOOD FOR THOUGHT

Paella is typically made in large pans and is meant to serve many people, almost as if from a bottomless pan of comfort food. My original recipe was adequate for 12 or more, so when I began adjusting it specifically for two people, I really had to scale down the ingredients in order to both make them fit into a 10-inch sauté pan, but also for the total volume of the recipe so you wouldn't be eating leftover paella for a week (as good as this dish is, that's overkill). Because my *Stove-Top Paella* calls for just half each of a yellow pepper, orange pepper, and graffiti eggplant, I decided to turn the remaining halves into my *Vegetable & Arugula Tacos* (page 205). It always amazes me how the same vegetables can be made into such incredibly different dishes from one another! There is simply nothing better in life than delicious options.

INGREDIENTS & PREP

Water – ¼ cup, hot from the tap

Saffron Threads – ½ teaspoon

Olive Oil – 4 tablespoons

Orange Pepper – ½ medium, ½-inch diced

Yellow Pepper – ½ medium, ½-inch diced

Red Onion – ½ medium, ½-inch diced

Graffiti Eggplant – ½ medium, ½-inch diced

Garlic – 3 cloves, finely minced

Italian Arborio Rice – ⅔ cup

Tomato Paste – 1 tablespoon

Lemon Zest – 1 teaspoon, freshly zested, divided

White Wine – ¼ cup (a dry variety)

Vegetable Stock – 1¼ cups

Sea Salt – ½ teaspoon

Black Pepper – ½ teaspoon, freshly cracked

Smoked Paprika – ½ teaspoon

Cherry Tomatoes – 1 cup, halved lengthwise

Green Peas – ⅔ cup frozen, thawed

Capers – 2 tablespoons, drained

Scallions – 2 tablespoons, thinly sliced, white and light green parts

Parsley – 3 tablespoons, fresh, roughly chopped (Italian flat leaf parsley recommended)

PLANNING

Yield – serves 2

MAIN COURSES

Sweet Potato Curry

SAVORY, SWEET, AND A TAD BIT SPICY!

DIRECTIONS

1. Pre-heat the oven to 425 degrees F.

2. Place the sweet potatoes onto a sheet pan and toss with 1 tablespoon of oil olive, ¼ teaspoon of salt, and ¼ teaspoon of pepper. Roast for 20-25 minutes until the edges are caramelized, tossing once half way through the roasting time.

3. Meanwhile, in a 10-inch sauté pan set over medium heat, add 1 tablespoon of olive oil. Once hot, add the red onions, red peppers, and red pepper flakes. Cook for 8-10 minutes, or until the onions and peppers are tender, stirring occasionally. Add the garlic and cook for another 1 minute, being careful not to burn the garlic.

4. Next, to the sauté pan, add the tomatoes, peas, half & half, curry powder, turmeric, cumin, honey, ¾ teaspoon of salt, and ¾ teaspoon of pepper.

5. Allow to come to a simmer, reduce the heat to low, and cook for 10 minutes.

6. Next, carefully stir in the roasted sweet potatoes and Paneer cheese. Allow to continue to simmer for another 5 minutes.

7. Transfer to a large serving bowl, garnish with fresh parsley, and serve immediately.

TIP
My *Sweet Potato Curry* pairs nicely with Basmati rice. For a healthy alternative, serve it with a fresh green salad or thick-cut cucumber slices.

INGREDIENTS & PREP

Sweet Potatoes - 1 large, peeled, ½-inch diced

Olive Oil - 2 tablespoons, divided

Sea Salt - 1 teaspoon, divided

Black Pepper - 1 teaspoon, freshly cracked, divided

Red Onion - ½ small, ½-inch diced

Red Pepper - 1 medium, ½-inch diced

Red Pepper Flakes - ¼ teaspoon

Garlic - 2 cloves, finely minced

Fire Roasted Tomatoes - 1 can (15 ounces)

Green Peas - ½ cup, frozen

Half & Half - ¼ cup

Yellow Curry Powder - 1¼ teaspoons

Turmeric - ¼ teaspoon

Cumin - ½ teaspoon

Honey - 2 teaspoons

Paneer Cheese - ⅓ pound, ½-inch diced

Parsley - ¼ cup, fresh, roughly chopped (Italian flat leaf parsley recommended)

PLANNING

Bake - 20-25 minutes, at 425 degrees F

Yield - serves 2

NOTES

_____

_____

_____

_____

_____

MAIN COURSES

Truffled Toast *with* Asparagus

AN ELEGANT INTERPRETATION OF A FAB DISH FROM A FAVORITE CHICAGO RESTAURANT!

DIRECTIONS

① Pre-heat the oven to 400 degrees F. Place two individual gratin dishes (6-7 inches in diameter) onto a half sheet pan.

② Place a slice of bread into each dish. Make an oval-shaped well in the center of each slice by removing bread about ½-inch deep.

③ Brush the tops of each slice with 3 tablespoons of truffle oil, allowing the bread to absorb the oil completely.

④ Place the half sheet pan with the gratin dishes and bread in the oven and bake for 6-8 minutes, or until the top of the bread is lightly toasted.

⑤ Meanwhile, in a 10-inch sauté pan set over medium heat, add the butter and olive oil. Once hot, add the asparagus, salt, and pepper. Cook for 3 minutes, stirring occasionally.

⑥ Next, add the garlic and continue cooking for another 1 minute, being careful not to burn the garlic. Then, remove from the heat, transfer into a small bowl, and set aside.

⑦ Once the bread has finished baking, remove the sheet pan from the oven, and top each slice evenly with both cheeses. Next, gently place two eggs yolks into the well of each slice, being careful not to break the yolks, and then evenly distribute the asparagus mixture all over and around the bread.

⑧ Return the sheet pan to the oven and bake for just another 1 minute, until the cheese is just slightly melted. The egg yolks will still be raw and runny.

⑨ Remove from the oven, and garnish with more salt and pepper to taste. Serve immediately.

Tip: When your knife and fork cut into the bread and pierce the warmed but raw egg yolks, you start to make the fabulous "sauce" of this dish as it mixes with the cheese and asparagus. The fresher the eggs, the more flavor!

INGREDIENTS & PREP

Challah Bread – 2 slices, cut 2-inches thick

Truffle Oil – 6 tablespoons

Butter – 1 tablespoon, unsalted

Olive Oil – 1 tablespoon

Asparagus – 5 stalks, bottom ends trimmed and discarded, cut ¾-inch on the diagonal, tips included

Sea Salt – ¼ teaspoon

Black Pepper – ¼ teaspoon

Garlic – 2 cloves, thinly sliced

Fontina Cheese – ½ cup, freshly grated

Pecorino Cheese – ¼ cup, freshly grated

Egg Yolks – 4 extra-large, whole, at room temperature, separated into 2 bowls

PLANNING

Bake – 10 minutes, at 400 degrees F

Yield – serves 2

A LITTLE STORY

My apartment building was constructed in 1924, and was originally built as a hotel. While it has been a residential building for a few years now, an amenity from its days as a storied hotel (competing only with The Drake) still remain: An Italian restaurant on the former lobby level. It is a wickedly short elevator ride from my apartment, and the wine bar downstairs is the perfect spot to meet Ryan on his way into the building from work to share a dish and glass of wine while we talk about our days and unwind for the evening. One of our favorite dishes from the wine bar inspired my *Truffled Toast with Asparagus* and is now a favorite at home!

MAIN COURSES

Vegetable & Arugula Tacos
SPICY AND FRESH FLAVORS ENVELOPED IN A GOAT CHEESE CREMA!

DIRECTIONS

GOAT CHEESE CREMA
1. Add all of the ingredients into a medium bowl and whisk until completely smooth. Set aside.

VEGETABLE & ARUGULA TACOS
2. In a 10-inch sauté pan set over medium-low heat, add the olive oil. Once hot, add the fennel, orange and yellow peppers, red onion, and eggplant. Cook for 12-14 minutes, stirring occasionally, until the vegetables are very tender, but not browned.

3. Next, to the sauté pan, add the salt, black pepper, garlic, paprika, chili powder, chipotle pepper, and scallions. Cook for another 1 minute, being careful not to burn the garlic.

4. Transfer to a medium bowl and stir in the arugula and basil.

ASSEMBLY
5. Evenly spoon the mixture into the taco shells, garnish with fresh chives, and the Goat Cheese Crema. Serve.

TIP
I typically serve my *Vegetable & Arugula Tacos* on a big plater with extra arugula and Goat Cheese Crema on the side. You can also serve with guacamole, fresh tomatoes, shredded red cabbage, and wedges of lime on the side as well! Also, use the remaining half each of the yellow and orange peppers, and the eggplant, in my *Stove-Top Paella* (page 199).

IDEA
Chipotle Pepper is potent – so start out with just ⅛ teaspoon and go from there! It may not seem like a lot, but trust me, it does add some heat. Chipotle Pepper is only one ingredient: Dried, smoked jalapeño peppers that are then crushed into a powder. It has a richly smoky-sweet flavor, and is typical in Southwest and Mexican cooking. Or, in this case, Mexican-inspired cooking!

INGREDIENTS & PREP

GOAT CHEESE CREMA
Goat Cheese – 3 ounces

Crème Fraîche – 1 tablespoon

Half & Half – 1½ tablespoons

Lime Zest – ⅛ teaspoon, freshly zested

Cayenne Pepper – ⅛ teaspoon

Cumin – ⅛ teaspoon

Sea Salt – ⅛ teaspoon

VEGETABLE & ARUGULA TACOS
Olive Oil – 3 tablespoons

Fennel – ½ large bulb, core removed and discarded, ¼-inch diced

Orange Pepper – ½ medium, ¼-inch diced

Yellow Pepper – ½ medium, ¼-inch diced

Red Onion – ½ medium, ¼-inch diced

Graffiti Eggplant – ½ medium, ¼-inch diced

Sea Salt – ½ teaspoon

Black Pepper – ½ teaspoon

Garlic – 2 cloves, finely minced

Smoked Paprika – ½ teaspoon

Chili Powder – ½ teaspoon

Chipotle Pepper – ⅛ teaspoon

Scallions – 1½ tablespoons, white and light green parts, finely minced

Arugula – ½ cup

Basil – 2 tablespoons, fresh, finely minced

Chives – 2 tablespoons, fresh, thinly sliced

Taco Shells – 6

PLANNING
Yield – makes 6 tacos

MAIN COURSES

Vietnamese-Inspired Pho

TRULY GLOBAL CUISINE—A VIETNAMESE DISH, BY WAY OF HAWAII, CREATED IN CHICAGO

DIRECTIONS

① Line a half sheet pan with a baking rack. Place 1 cup of corn starch in a medium sized bowl. Place the other ½ cup on a large plate and spread into an even layer. Set each step aside.

② Line another plate with a double layer of paper towels. Place the tofu cubes, in a single layer, onto the plate. Cover them with another double layer of paper towels. Gently press to help dry the tofu. Allow to sit for 10 minutes. You may have to switch out the top layer of paper towels once during this process.

③ Meanwhile, in a medium sauce pan set over high heat, add the canola oil. Heat until the oil reaches 350 degrees F (use a candy thermometer to be accurate).

④ After the tofu is mostly dry, toss the cubes into the bowl of corn starch to coat evenly and completely. Once coated, place the tofu cubes onto the plate with the corn starch.

⑤ Once the oil has reached 350 degrees F, and working with three batches of tofu cubes, gently place the first batch of tofu in the oil and fry until golden brown, about 8-10 minutes. Remove the tofu from the hot oil with a slotted spoon and place onto the prepared half sheet pan to drain. Repeat these steps with next two batches until all of the tofu has been fried.

⑥ Meanwhile, while the batches of tofu are frying, in a large stock pot, bring the vegetable stock to a boil.

⑦ In the boiling vegetable stock, cook the prepared cauliflower and carrots for 3-5 minutes, or until just tender. Using a slotted spoon, remove and drain the vegetables, and place into a bowl. Set aside (They should still have a bit of a bite to them as this will give the soup a wonderful texture).

⑧ Once all the tofu has been fried and set aside, place the rice noodles in the vegetable stock and cook according to the package directions. When the noodles have finished cooking, evenly divide the noodles and the stock into two large bowls.

⑨ Lastly, place half each of the tofu, cauliflower, carrots, basil, lime wedges, uncooked corn, and uncooked garlic into each bowl, keeping each ingredient in a group. Garnish with hot chili sauce and scallions. Serve immediately.

INGREDIENTS & PREP

Corn Starch - 1½ cups

Tofu - 1 block (12 ounces), very firm, cut into ¾-inch cubes

Canola Oil - 3½ cups

Vegetable Stock - 8 cups

Cauliflower - 1 bag (14 ounces), frozen, florets

Carrot - 1 cup, peeled, sliced ⅛-inch thick

Rice Noodles - 4 ounces (Vermicelli-style recommended)

Basil - ½ cup, fresh, whole leaves

Lime - 1 small, cut into eighths

Sweet Corn - 1 medium ear, kernels only

Garlic - 2 cloves, thinly sliced

Sriracha Hot Chili Sauce - to taste, for garnish

Scallions - ¼ cup, white and light green parts, thinly sliced

PLANNING

Yield - serves 2

A LITTLE STORY

My *Vietnamese-Inspired Pho* is a little nod to my favorite Vietnamese restaurant in Honolulu's Chinatown, which happens to make my most favorite pho, ever! While mine isn't a traditional pho, it certainly curbs my cravings back home in Chicago!

DESSERTS

Desserts
THE PERFECT ENDING FOR ANY OCCASION

Brown Sugar Ice Cream, 211

Chewy Coconut Cookies, 213

Crème Brûlée with Honey & Lemon, 215

Drunken Pineapple with Sweet Cream, 217

Maple & Orange Madeleines, 219

Peach & Plum Crisp, 221

Petit S'mores Croissants, 223

Shortbread Truffles, 225

Sparkling Raspberry Sorbet, 227

Store-Bought Cake Made Fabulous!, 229

Warm Chocolate Pots with Grand Marnier & Cherries, 231

The Peanut Butter Puppenheimer (for your +1 pup), 233

DESSERTS

Brown Sugar Ice Cream
I SCREAM, YOU SCREAM, WE ALL SCREAM FOR *THIS* ICE CREAM!

DIRECTIONS

① In a medium sauce pan set over medium heat, add the heavy cream, sugar, salt, and vanilla. Stir until the sugar is just dissolved, about 5 minutes. You can tell the sugar is dissolved by rubbing a bit of the cream between your fingertips. If there are no granulates, it is done.

② Transfer to a bowl and cover with plastic wrap, pressing it directly onto the surface of the mixture. Chill until very cold, or overnight.

③ Once the mixture is very cold, add it to an ice cream maker and follow the manufacturer's directions.

④ You can either serve the ice cream once it has finished churning, or place it in an air-tight container and freeze for up to 1 week.

INGREDIENTS & PREP

Heavy Cream - 3 cups

Dark Brown Sugar - ⅔ cups, lightly packed

Fleur de Sel - ¼ teaspoon

Vanilla - 1 teaspoon, pure extract

PLANNING

Yield - makes 1 quart

TIP
If you make my *Brown Sugar Ice Cream* ahead of time, allow it to sit at room temperature for 5-10 minutes before serving. This will ensure the ice cream has a creamier texture and will allow the flavors to come through even more!

FOOD FOR THOUGHT
My *Brown Sugar Ice Cream* has a very subtle caramel flavor from the dark brown sugar, and when combined with the vanilla, salt, and richness of the cream, it reminds me of a salted caramel ice cream. Serve this ice cream whenever you would typically serve a plain vanilla ice cream since it has over-the-top flavor. You can also garnish with warm salted caramel sauce (your favorite store-bought brand is easy enough), or crumbled shortbread cookies, and even the **Homemade Whipped Sweet Cream** (page 229), for an unexpectedly easy and yet completely elegant dessert!

NOTES

DESSERTS

Chewy Coconut Cookies

MOVE OVER MACAROONS, THERE IS A NEW COOKIE IN TOWN!

DIRECTIONS

1. Pre-heat the oven to 350 degrees F. Line a half sheet pan with parchment paper. Set aside.

2. In a medium bowl, add the coconut, flour, and salt. Stir until all of the coconut is coated with flour.

3. Next, add the vanilla, honey, and condensed milk. Stir until completely incorporated.

4. Scoop 2 rounded tablespoons of the mixture onto the prepared sheet pan, leaving about 2 inches between each cookie.

5. Bake for 15-17 minutes, until the edges are golden brown.

6. Remove from the oven and transfer the cookies to a wire rack to cool for 20 minutes before serving.

TIP
Because my *Chewy Coconut Cookies* can be prepared so quickly, I love to make these just before I am going to serve them. They are so tender when they are fresh and have the most incredible texture, not to mention make the entire house smell like a bakery!

IDEA
I love this cookie for dessert but also to serve along with my *Lavender Earl Grey Tea* (page 79), either in the morning as a sweet treat, or as part of afternoon tea. This recipe doubles easily and I sometimes like to send my +1 home with a little cookie "goodie" bag as a take-away gift!

FOOD FOR THOUGHT
While the ingredients of my *Chewy Coconut Cookies* are almost the same as a traditional Coconut Macaroon, they have a completely different look and texture – which is why I think this recipe is one to keep at the ready when you want to serve something as simple as a cookie, but with a twist! These are very dense, chewy, but still light, and have such fabulous flavor. The addition of the honey really adds a warmth and helps to round-out the other sweetness in the coconut and condensed milk.

INGREDIENTS & PREP

Sweetened Shredded Coconut - 1¼ cups

Flour - ¼ cup

Sea Salt - ⅛ teaspoon

Vanilla - ¾ teaspoon

Honey - 2 tablespoons

Sweetened Condensed Milk - ½ cup

PLANNING

Bake - 15-17 minutes, at 350 degrees F

Yield - makes 8 cookies

NOTES

DESSERTS

Crème Brûlée *with* Honey & Lemon
THIS CLASSIC DESSERT HAS A STUNNING REMAKE WITH CRÈME FRAÎCHE

DIRECTIONS

① Pre-heat the oven to 300 degrees F. Place 2 individual ramekins (4-5 ounces each) into an 8x8 baking dish. Set aside.

② In a small sauce pan set over medium heat, add the heavy cream, crème fraîche, vanilla, honey, and salt. Stir to combine ingredients. Bring to just under the simmering point and then remove from the heat.

③ Meanwhile, in the bowl of an electric mixer fitted with the paddle attachment, add the yolks, sugar, and lemon zest. Mix on low speed until just combined.

④ Once the cream mixture is hot, and with the mixer still on low speed, very slowly pour the hot cream mixture into the yolk mixture. Mix until just combined.

⑤ Evenly pour the custard into the ramekins. Then, into the baking dish, pour enough hot tap water to go half way up the sides of the ramekins.

⑥ Carefully transfer the baking dish into the oven, and bake for 30-35 minutes, until the custard is set.

⑦ Remove the ramekins from the water bath and allow to cool at room temperature. Once cooled, transfer them to the refrigerator to chill for at least 2 hours.

⑧ When you are ready to serve, remove the ramekins from the refrigerator and sprinkle the tops of the custards with sugar (approximately 2 teaspoons for each). Use either a small kitchen torch or a very hot broiler and brûlée the sugar until it caramelizes and turns a deep golden brown, being careful not to burn the sugar (if using a broiler be sure the heat caramelizes the sugar evenly – you may need to shift the ramekins once or twice).

Tip: Traditionally, crème brûlée is served chilled with a caramelized sugar top. However, you can also caramelize the tops while the custards are still warm and enjoy this dessert warm – for some reason I think it seems wonderfully indulgent.

INGREDIENTS & PREP

Heavy Cream – ¾ cup

Crème Fraîche – ¾ cup

Vanilla – ¼ teaspoon

Honey – 1 tablespoon

Sea Salt – ⅛ teaspoon

Egg Yolks – 3 extra-large, at room temperature

Sugar – 2½ tablespoons, plus more for serving

Lemon Zest – ¾ teaspoon, freshly zested

PLANNING

Bake – 30-35 minutes, at 300 degrees F

Yield – serves 2

FOOD FOR THOUGHT

I chose to include my version of this iconic dessert here because it has a twist worthy of being at a table just for two! I have had crème brûlées with weird combinations of flavors, trying to be edgy, but the beauty of the classic version is just how simple it is. And that is what makes my *Crème Brûlée with Honey & Lemon* work so well—my "remake" involves everyday ingredients like honey, lemon, and tart crème fraîche that enhance the classic flavors instead of overwhelming them. Honey and lemon are like secret-weapon ingredients to me, I use them both in sweet and savory cooking for their complexity that enhances, but doesn't overpower. The addition of crème fraîche to this recipe not only adds extra silkiness to the custard, but also a little tartness, taking this classic dessert to the next level, all with ingredients that don't require extraordinary explanation!

DESSERTS

Drunken Pineapple *with* Sweet Cream

THIS COMBINATION OF FRUIT AND BOOZE MAKES FOR A FABULOUS AFTER-DINNER TREAT!

DIRECTIONS

DRUNKEN PINEAPPLE

1. In a medium sauce pan set over low heat, add the rum, honey, sugar, and salt. Heat until the sugar is dissolved, about 5 minutes, stirring occasionally.

2. Transfer to a medium bowl and add the diced pineapple. Stir to combine. Cover and allow to sit at room temperature for at least 8 hours, or overnight.

SWEET WHIPPED CREAM

3. Combine all of the ingredients for the whipped cream into a medium bowl. Whisk until it thickens, about 5 minutes.

TO SERVE

4. When you are ready to serve, make the *Sweet Whipped Cream*. Set aside.

5. In a small sauce pan set over medium heat, add the pineapple and the liquid. Heat until warm, but not hot.

6. Using a slotted spoon, spoon the pineapple evenly into 2 bowls. Top each with *Sweet Whipped Cream* and serve.

INGREDIENTS & PREP

DRUNKEN PINEAPPLE

Dark Rum – ¼ cup

Honey – 3 tablespoons

Dark Brown Sugar – 3 tablespoons

Sea Salt – ⅛ teaspoon

Pineapple – 12 ounces, fresh, 1-inch diced

SWEET WHIPPED CREAM

Mascarpone – ¼ cup

Crème Fraîche – 2 tablespoons

Heavy Cream – 1 tablespoon

Honey – 1 tablespoon

PLANNING

Prep Time – marinate for 8 hours, or overnight

Yield – serves 2

IDEA

Once you have removed the warm pineapple from the saucepan, strain the liquid through a fine mesh sieve into a glass measuring cup. Pour the warm boozy liquid into small snifters or cordial glasses and serve as a "chaser" with dessert!

NOTES

DESSERTS

m

Maple & Orange Madeleines
LITTLE CAKES THAT ARE SOAKED IN DARK MAPLE SYRUP

DIRECTIONS

1. Pre-heat the oven to 350 degrees F. Butter and flour a standard sized madeleine pan. Set aside.

2. Start by sifting the flour, baking powder, and salt into a small bowl. Set aside.

3. In the bowl of an electric mixer fitted with a paddle attachment, beat the eggs, vanilla extract, and orange zest on high speed until it thickens, about 5 minutes.

4. Reduce the speed to medium, and gradually add the powdered sugar and beat for an additional 5 minutes.

5. Turn off the mixer and gently fold in the flour mixture, then the melted butter. Mix until smooth.

6. Spoon the batter into the wells of the pan, filling each about ¾ full.

7. Bake for 8-10 minutes, or until the edges are browned. Remove the pan from the oven and allow the cakes to cool for 3 minutes in the pan. Then, remove the cakes and place onto a wire rack, with their fluted sides down, and evenly spoon over the warm maple syrup.

8. Serve warm or at room temperature.

INGREDIENTS & PREP

Flour - ⅓ cup, all-purpose, plus more for dusting the pan

Baking Powder - ¼ teaspoon

Sea Salt - ⅛ teaspoon

Eggs - 1 extra-large, at room temperature

Vanilla - ½ teaspoon, pure extract

Orange Zest - 2 teaspoons, freshly zested

Powdered Sugar - ½ cup

Butter - 4 tablespoons, unsalted, melted and cooled, plus extra for greasing the pan

Maple Syrup - 8 tablespoons, warm, Grade A

PLANNING

Bake - 8-10 minutes, at 350 degrees F

Yield - makes 8 cakes

FOOD FOR THOUGHT

Madeleines are small sponge cakes with a distinctive shell-like shape which comes from baking in pans with shell-shaped wells. There are so many variations available, both in books and in bakeries. I haven't seen anything quite like my *Maple & Orange Madeleines*, with freshly grated orange zest in the batter, and infused with warm maple syrup when they are fresh from the oven. These little pillowy cakes are wonderfully distinctive and are a scrumptious compliment to my *Classic Champagne Elixirs* (page 95), or even my *Lavender Earl Grey Tea* (page 79).

NOTES

_____

_____

_____

_____

_____

_____

_____

DESSERTS

Peach & Plum Crisp

BE CAREFUL, THIS DESSERT MAY STEAL THE SHOW—IT IS JUST THAT GOOD!

DIRECTIONS

① Pre-heat the oven to 375 degrees F. Butter a gratin dish or other oven-proof dish, roughly 1½ quarts, and place it on a half sheet pan lined with parchment paper. Set aside.

CRUMB TOPPING

② Place all of the ingredients into the bowl of an electric mixer fitted with a paddle attachment. Mix on low speed until the butter is in small pieces, about the size of peas, about 5 minutes. Turn off the mixer and set aside.

FILLING

③ In a medium bowl, add the fruit, sugar, honey, and flour. Gently toss to evenly combine and coat the fruit.

ASSEMBLY

④ Pour the fruit mixture into the prepared gratin dish.

⑤ Next, evenly top the fruit mixture with the crumb topping.

⑥ Bake for 35-40 minutes, or until the top is golden brown and the sides are bubbling. Remove from the oven and allow to cool for 10 minutes before serving.

MASCARPONE DRIZZLE

⑦ As the crisp is cooling, prepare the mascarpone drizzle.

⑧ Add both ingredients to a small bowl and whisk until smooth.

⑨ As you plate each serving of the crisp, top each with the mascarpone drizzle to taste, and serve.

INGREDIENTS & PREP

CRUMB TOPPING

Sugar - 3 tablespoons

Dark Brown Sugar - 3 tablespoons

Flour - ⅓ cup

Old-Fashioned Rolled Oats - ⅓ cup

Sea Salt - ⅛ teaspoon

Butter - 4 tablespoons, very cold, diced, unsalted

FILLING

Peaches - 2, fresh, pitted, cut into 8 wedges

Plums - 3, fresh, pitted, cut into 8 wedges

Raspberries - 1 cup, fresh

Sugar - ¼ cup

Honey - 2 tablespoons

Flour - 2 tablespoons, all-purpose

MASCARPONE DRIZZLE

Mascarpone - ¼ cup

Heavy Cream - 1 tablespoon

PLANNING

Bake - 35-40 minutes, at 375 degrees F

Yield - serves 2

IDEA

If you don't have a stand mixer, you can make my *Peach & Plum Crisp* the old fashioned way - it is worth it! I can remember my nan in the kitchen making a crumbled topping using two butter knives to blend the dry ingredients into the butter. She would run the blades of the knives cross-wise from one another to cut the butter into small pieces that make the crumb topping work. The same was true when she made pie dough. The sound of the steel knives against the glass bowl always ran shivers down my back, but at the same time got me excited with anticipation for what was going to come out of her oven!

DESSERTS

Petit S'mores Croissants
A CHILDHOOD FAVORITE WORTHY OF THE CHICEST PARTY

DIRECTIONS

① Pre-heat the oven to 350 degrees F. Take 3 squares of aluminum foil, 12-inches across, and cut them in half on the diagonal. Line a half sheet pan with parchment paper. Slice each croissant horizontally along the outside curve, careful not to cut all the way through—you want to make a "pocket" for the filling to nestle into. Set all three steps aside.

② Next, fill the pocket created in each croissant with a half sheet of graham cracker, then evenly fill with the chocolate and marshmallows. Evenly sprinkle the inside of the filled croissants with fleur de sel.

③ Place each stuffed croissant in the center of an aluminum foil triangle and wrap each croissant loosely in a foil pocket – be sure the ends are sealed.

④ Place all six wrapped croissants onto the prepared sheet pan. Bake for 20 minutes.

⑤ Remove from the oven and place onto a serving platter and serve hot.

Tip: Instead of using a half sheet pan for baking, you can also use a small cast iron skillet, or another oven-proof baking dish – and go right from the oven to the table (remember a trivet)!

INGREDIENTS & PREP

Mini Croissants - 6, freshly baked, store-bought

Graham Crackers - 3 full sheets, halved

Semi-Sweet Chocolate - 2 ounces, broken into small pieces (Ghirardelli brand recommended)

Mini Marshmallows - ¾ cup

Fleur de Sel - ⅛ teaspoon

PLANNING

Bake - 20 minutes, at 350 degrees F

Yield - serves 2

NOTES

_____
_____
_____
_____
_____
_____
_____

A LITTLE STORY

When I was little, nan would make me s'mores in the oven. She would start by layering Hersey's chocolate squares and giant marshmallows between two squares of graham crackers, then she would wrap those in aluminum foil and bake them in the oven. We would burn our fingers impatiently trying to tear open the hot foil, and then burn our mouths on the ooey-gooey chocolate are marshmallow oozing from the graham crackers. But, they were always fun to make, and they were always a treat to eat! I think we tried (a few times!) roasting marshmallows over the open flame of the stove's burners, and that just made a giant mess. When I was putting together the final list of desserts for this book, I really wanted to include something that had a "high and low" appeal. S'mores are childhood goodness and as simple as it gets. Involving mini croissant, with their buttery flakiness was the "haute" I needed. I think stuffing mini croissants with the fixin's for s'mores is just fabulous, quirky, and unexpected. This can best be seen in the reaction of your guests when you serve a dish of what looks like a fancy or complicated dish prepared in aluminum foil, and they unwrap my Petit S'mores Croissants to realize they get to sink their teeth into the simple, yet elevated, deliciousness of s'mores!

DESSERTS

Shortbread Truffles
LITTLE BITES OF SWEET BLISS

DIRECTIONS

1. Place the white chocolate, vanilla bean paste, and cinnamon into a medium bowl and set aside.

2. In a small sauce pan set over medium heat, add the cream, honey, and fleur de sel. Bring to just under the simmering point. Remove from the heat and pour over the white chocolate. Stir until completely smooth to create the ganache.

3. Cover the ganache tightly with plastic wrap and place into the refrigerator for 1 hour, or until firm.

4. In the bowl of a small food processor fitted with a steel blade, add the shortbread cookies. Pulse until finely ground. Transfer to a shallow dish. Line a half sheet pan with parchment paper. Set both steps aside.

5. Using a 1-inch scoop or tablespoon, scoop out balls of ganache and place onto the prepared sheet pan.

6. After you have scooped all the ganache, roll each ball by hand to form a truffle (they do not have to be perfectly round!), and then roll each truffle through the ground shortbread cookies to coat evenly all around.

7. Place on a serving dish and serve immediately.

INGREDIENTS & PREP

White Chocolate - 4 ounces, very finely chopped

Vanilla Bean Paste - ¼ teaspoon

Cinnamon - ¼ teaspoon

Heavy Cream - 1 tablespoon

Honey - 2 teaspoons

Fleur de Sel - ⅛ teaspoon

Shortbread Cookies - 3 ounces, store-bought

PLANNING

Yield - makes 8-10 truffles

NOTES

A LITTLE STORY

Whenever I serve truffles for dessert, people are so often mesmerized when I say, "I made these myself!" In fact, truffles are incredibly simple to make at home and without the use of any specialty kitchen equipment. And there are simply endless flavor combinations! In my first cookbook *Entertaining with Love*, I included my signature recipe for *Honey Lavender Milk Chocolate Truffles*. Since its debut in 2012, I have made close to fifteen thousand of them for gifts, client parties, and even for sale on my website – each one made by me! They're that easy. What I love about truffles is they are so elegant and make people feel very special! Typically, milk or dark chocolate truffles are rolled in luscious cocoa powder, which gives them even more chocolaty flavor. My *Shortbread Truffles* are made with white chocolate and since there isn't such a thing as "white chocolate cocoa powder" (just a hot chocolate mix), I wanted something to roll them in that would add flavor and help enhance the white chocolate. I tried many different things, but settled on very finely ground shortbread cookies. The shortbread compliments the white chocolate, vanilla, and cinnamon, and adds a subtle buttery flavor – need I say more?!

DESSERTS

Sparkling Raspberry Sorbet
SWEET, TART, AND BUBBLY—THE PERFECT DESSERT COMBO!

DIRECTIONS

FOUR BERRY SAUCE

1. In a small saucepan set over medium heat, add the frozen berries, preserves, liqueur, and lemon zest.

2. Cook for 10-15 minutes, until the berries have released their juices and are very tender, stirring occasionally. Remove from heat.

3. Place a fine mesh sieve over a glass bowl. Transfer the mixture into the sieve.

4. Using the back of a wooden spoon press the mixture through the sieve.

5. Cover tightly with plastic wrap and refrigerate until chilled.

TO SERVE

6. Layer this luscious berry sauce in a small coupe with a single scoop of raspberry sorbet and ¼ cup of very dry, chilled Champagne. It is a perfect dessert for a grown-up celebration, very elegant presentation, and just an all-around fabulous surprise for your guests.

INGREDIENTS & PREP

FOUR BERRY SAUCE

Frozen Berry Medley – 1 pound, raspberries, strawberries, blackberries, and blueberries

Raspberry Preserves – 2 tablespoons

Raspberry Liqueur – 1 tablespoon (Chambord® recommended)

Lemon Zest – 1 teaspoon, freshly zested

COMPONENTS

Raspberry Sorbet – 1 pint, store-bought (your favorite variety)

Champagne – 1 bottle, 750mL, very chilled (Dry or Brut recommended)

PLANNING

Yield – makes 1½ cups

FOOD FOR THOUGHT

It is no secret I love to entertain at home! From menu planning, to setting the table, or spending time in my kitchen, I will find any excuse to throw a soirée! While I certainly have a few tricks up my sleeve to ensure my guests are always having a fabulous time, one of my top tips, which equally applies when entertaining just for your plus-one, is to never make everything yourself. I like to choose two or three different dishes to prepare, then rely on favorite store-bought brands, bakeries, and gourmet markets to round out my menu. It's the simplest way to ensure that I can focus on the menu items that I want to make, and still have a fabulous time entertaining!

They say the dessert is what people always remember from any party. A really good dessert is always something I like to pay special attention to. Whether I am making it myself, or heading to one of my neighborhood bakeries (for my *Store-Bought Cake Made Fabulous*, page 229), I make sure to always have something that will have a "*Wow!*" factor. That is exactly what my *Sparking Raspberry Sorbet* will do for your final course. This particular dessert relies on simple components: Your favorite Champagne, really good store-bought Raspberry Sorbet, and the most flavorful homemade *Four Berry Sauce*.

Besides being a perfectly elegant dessert for any occasion, it is one of the easiest desserts to assemble. Once you make the *Four Berry Sauce* (which uses frozen berries and can be stored in the refrigerator), it all comes together in just a few minutes! I love to serve this in a small coupe, small bowl, or even in a martini glass. Bottoms (and spoons!) up!

DESSERTS

m

Store-Bought Cake Made Fabulous!
VERY EASY AND STRESS-FREE IDEAS TO "ZHUSH" A SIMPLE CAKE

THE CAKE
First, the word "zhush" means to make something exciting or more attractive, or to make it more fabulous (at least, that is how I use it!). This highly technical term can really be used to describe a lot of different scenarios, but in this case, it is all about saving time by making a plain, simple, store-bought cake fabulous! When I don't have the time to make a cake from scratch (or don't want to be bothered), I like to buy a small simple chocolate cake with chocolate buttercream to zhush up and turn it into something I am not only excited about serving, but also eating! Grocery store bakeries are usually filled with cakes ranging in size and expense. My approach for a *Store-Bought Cake Made Fabulous!* is to buy the simplest and most delicious cake I can find. Save yourself the silly sprinkles, overly sugary buttercream roses, or that really creepy plastic clown holding balloons (which, I think we have all had at some for a childhood birthday at some point!). Instead of relying of those pre-fab decorated cakes, focus on quality, and use these simple options to dress up even the most unassuming store-bought cake:

EDIBLE FLOWERS
Colorful edible flowers, which are typically in the produce department of many grocery stores, makes for a casual yet unexpected and elegant effect. I love dusting them with a bit of powdered sugar to help sweeten them (they are *very* earthy tasting), and to add a bit of texture and contrast. This is especially elegant on larger edible rose petals!

HOMEMADE SWEETENED WHIPPED CREAM
Keep it simple and straight-forward with homemade sweetened whipped cream. In this case, there is no store-bought substitute. However, your electric mixer does all the work. This is also a wonderful decoration for almost any flavor of cake! I like to use a piping bag fitted with a large round tip (or a star tip) to pipe around the base of the cake where the cardboard disk meets the serving plate. To make homemade sweetened whipped cream you need:

INGREDIENTS & PREP
Heavy Cream – 1 cup, very cold

Sugar – 2 tablespoons

Vanilla – ¾ teaspoon, pure extract

EDIBLE GOLD LEAF
Believe me, you don't need a bank loan for this option, but it is a stunning way to decorate a cake! You can easily find edible gold leaf (and even silver) online or in specialty cake decorating shops. It comes in a pack of fine thin sheets, which you can keep on hand for any zhushing need. It adds a touch of glamour to fresh raspberries for this cake! The same would be true for strawberries, blackberries, or even blueberries. Choose a fresh berry or fruit that will complement the flavor of both the cake and frosting you choose.

STORE-BOUGHT SALTED CARAMEL
Simple store-bought salted caramel poured over the top of the cake, makes a truly decadent addition! When you slice into the cake, the caramel oozes down into the cake slices and makes each and every bite gooey and scrumptious. I usually keep a little extra caramel sauce on-hand to serve alongside the cake. For added fabulousness, you can also heat up the caramel and pour it over the cake as you present it. Or, add a touch more flaked sea salt for more flavor and crunch!

DIRECTIONS

1. In the bowl of an electric mixer fitted with a whisk attachment, add the cold cream. Turn the mixer to medium-low and begin whipping the cream. Once it starts to thicken, add the sugar and vanilla.

2. Raise the speed to high, and whip it until it thickens and begins to form medium peaks. It should be a bit "soft" as the texture is airier and much creamier.

DESSERTS

Warm Chocolate Pots *with* Grand Marnier & Cherries
AN INDULGENT AND ELEGANT DESSERT MADE WITH A FEW SIMPLE INGREDIENTS

DIRECTIONS

1. Start by pre-heating the oven to 425 degrees F.

2. Butter the interior of two ramekins (6 to 8 ounces each) and place on a baking dish. Set aside.

3. In a heat-proof bowl set over barely simmering water, melt the chocolate and butter, stirring occasionally until just melted. Remove the bowl from the heat.

4. Next, to the chocolate, add the orange liqueur, salt, powdered sugar, cocoa powder, and vanilla. Whisk until blended.

5. Slowly whisk in the eggs.

6. Toss the cherries with the flour, then stir into the chocolate mixture.

7. Lastly, evenly divide the batter into the prepared ramekins. Bake for exactly 15 minutes. Remove from the oven and allow to stand for 2 minutes. Garnish with cocoa powder and candied orange peel. Serve warm.

INGREDIENTS & PREP

Semi-Sweet Chocolate – 3½ ounces, roughly chopped

Butter – 4 tablespoons, unsalted, plus more for preparing ramekins

Orange Liqueur – 2 tablespoons (Grand Marnier® recommended)

Sea Salt – ¼ teaspoon

Powdered Sugar – ½ cup

Cocoa Powder – 1 tablespoon, plus more for dusting

Vanilla – 1 teaspoon, pure extract

Eggs – 1 extra-large, plus 1 extra-large egg yolk

Dried Cherries – ½ cup

Flour – 3 tablespoons

Candied Orange Peel – for garnish (optional)

PLANNING

Bake – 15 minutes, at 425 degrees F

Yield – serves 2

TIP
You can actually make these ahead of time! Bake and allow to cool completely. Then, wrap each one tightly with foil and place in the refrigerator. When it's time to serve, remove from the refrigerator 30 minutes prior. Discard the foil and warm in a microwave for 45 seconds. Dust with cocoa powder and serve immediately.

IDEA
You can also swap out the orange liqueur for Cabernet Sauvignon. In winter months I also like to add ⅛ teaspoon of cinnamon to give these little chocolate pots an extra zing!

NOTES

DESSERTS

The Peanut Butter Puppenheimer
COME! SIT! STAY! EAT!

DIRECTIONS

1. Pre-heat the oven to 375 degrees F. Line a sheet pan with parchment paper. Set aside.
2. In a medium bowl, mix together the banana, peanut butter, honey, and vegetable stock.
3. Add the flour and baking powder. Mix until just combined.
4. Place spoonfuls of batter, about 1 tablespoon each, onto the prepared baking sheet, spaced 2 inches apart.
5. Flatten in a crisscross pattern with a fork. Each cookie should be about ½-inch thick.
6. Bake for 16 minutes. Remove from the oven and transfer onto a cooling rack. Allow to cool completely.

INGREDIENTS & PREP

Banana - ½, peeled, mashed
Peanut Butter - ½ cup, smooth
Vegetable Stock - ½ cup, at room temperature
Honey - 1 tablespoon
Whole Wheat Flour - 1 cup
Baking Powder - 1½ teaspoons

PLANNING

Bake - 16 minutes, at 375 degrees F
Yield - makes 28-30 cookies

A LITTLE PUP *of a* STORY

There is nothing I love better than spoiling our little pup Lady von Puppenheimer with kisses, toys, and her favorite homemade dog treat - *The Peanut Butter Puppenheimer*! After spending years owning a luxury pet boutique and portrait studio, where I would cater to my four-legged clients (and their owners!), I never did find a softer dog treat that could so easily be broken in little pieces for small dogs.

I was determined to create the solution myself, in my own kitchen, and started developing and testing dog treats. I make these treats with 100% organic human-grade ingredients to ensure there are as healthy and delicious as can be. In fact, as they bake, they smell so good you'd swear they were a treat for yourself! These make a wonderful gift for your plus-one who is also a dog lover - just stack a few in a glycine bag and tie with a colorful ribbon. Just remember to let your plus-one know they are for their pup!

NOTES

Recipe Index

RECIPE INDEX

GOOD MORNING

Baked Eggs with Goat Cheese, 63

Banana & Maple Dutch-Flan, 65

Berry & Basil Compote, 67

Cinnamon Raisin French Toast with Apples & Mascarpone, 69

Earl Grey & Lemon Butter, 71

Easy Strawberry Muffins, 73

Fig & Cream Scones, 75

Homemade Granola, 77

Lavender Earl Grey Tea, 79

Stuffed Croissants with Spinach, 81

HORS D'OEUVRE & COCKTAILS

Amaretto Sour Martini, 85

Baguette Pizza Bites, 87

Baked Camembert with Pears & Maple, 89

Basil French 75, 91

Beet & Parsley Canapés, 93

Classic Champagne Elixirs, 95

Dried Mango with Whipped Avocado, 97

Fig & Goat Cheese Truffles, 99

Fried Blue Cheese Olives, 101

Herbes de Provence Popcorn, 103

Homemade Ricotta, 105

Pea & Lemon Tartine, 107

Rosé Sangria with Peaches & Rosemary, 109

Salt & Pepper Potato Chips with Blue Cheese, 111

Spiced Chickpeas, 113

Spicy Garlic Edamame, 115

St-Germain Margarita, 117

Sun Dried Tomato & White Bean Spread, 119

Sweet Potato & Triple Cream Brie Tartine, 121

Yogurt, Fresh Herb & Cucumber Dip, 123

SOUPS & SALADS

Artichoke & Tomato Salad, 127

Asparagus Soup, 129

Butternut Squash & Black Bean Soup, 131

French Bistro Vinaigrette, 133

Lentil Stew, 135

Matchstick Apple Salad, 137

Roasted Cauliflower Soup, 139

Roasted Fruit with Rosemary Vinaigrette, 141

Warm White Bean Salad, 143

RECIPE INDEX

SIDES

Apple & Blue Cheese Slaw, 147

Balsamic Roasted Pearl Onions, 149

Brussels Sprouts with Strawberries, 151

Carpaccio of Cucumber, 153

Corn Gratin with White Cheddar, 155

Crème Fraîche Glazed Root Vegetables, 157

Dried Figs & Warm Orzo, 159

Herbes de Provence Tomatoes, 161

Roasted Cauliflower with Curried Browned Butter, 163

Triple Cream Sweet Potato Wedges, 165

Zucchini & Potato Gratin, 167

MAIN COURSES

Apple & Herb Wellington, 171

Butternut Squash Medallions with Wilted Spinach, 173

Caramelized Onion & White Cheddar Mac 'n Cheese, 175

Chicago Sliders, 177

Cinnamon Raisin Grilled Cheese, 179

Country Frittata with Petite Salad, 181

Fennel & Red Pepper Risotto, 183

French Lentils with Apples & Beets, 185

Herbed Cannellini Bean "Meatballs", 187

Hot & Sour Coconut Noodles, 189

Orange & Rosemary Cream Sauce, 191

Pear & Onion Tart, 193

Quinoa with Fresh Herbs, 195

Savory Dutch-Flan with Golden Potatoes, 197

Stove-Top Paella, 199

Sweet Potato Curry, 201

Truffled Toast with Asparagus, 203

Vegetable & Arugula Tacos, 205

Vietnamese-Inspired Pho, 207

DESSERTS

Brown Sugar Ice Cream, 211

Chewy Coconut Cookies, 213

Crème Brûlée with Honey & Lemon, 215

Drunken Pineapple with Sweet Cream, 217

Maple & Orange Madeleines, 219

Peach & Plum Crisp, 221

Petit S'mores Croissants, 223

Shortbread Truffles, 225

Sparkling Raspberry Sorbet, 227

Store-Bought Cake Made Fabulous!, 229

Warm Chocolate Pots with Grand Marnier & Cherries, 231

The Peanut Butter Puppenheimer, 233

Notes & Guest Book

NOTES & GUEST BOOK

Notes

IT IS ALWAYS BEST TO WRITE IT DOWN THE FIRST TIME!

NOTES & GUEST BOOK

NOTES & GUEST BOOK

Guest Book

KEEP A RECORD OF YOUR SHENANIGANS!

DATE	GUEST	MENU & NOTES

NOTES & GUEST BOOK

DATE	GUEST	MENU & NOTES

ALSO BY MARC J. SIEVERS

Entertaining with Love—Inspired recipes for everyday entertaining

Visit marcsievers.com for more

CPSIA information can be obtained
at www.ICGtesting.com
Printed in the USA
LVHW07*2046280818
588160LV00003B/5/P